Points of Departure

442

442

84

305

x   +

3 45
7
315

300
270
300

900

920

Reece McGee
Purdue University

Points of Departure   Basic Concepts in Sociology

The Dryden Press Inc.
Hinsdale, Illinois

Copyright © 1972 by The Dryden Press Inc.
All rights reserved
Library of Congress Catalog Card Number: 72-189897
ISBN: 0-03-089038-1
Printed in the United States of America

To Caseyroo, Hannes, and Bits

Preface

Students are rarely consulted by teachers in the matter of textbook selection, generally because the teachers do not know who their students will be at the time they place their orders. Still, it is reasonable for students to wonder about the purpose of a book and why it was selected; and I believe it is more the author's job to answer these questions than it is the teacher's. My principal purpose in putting this book together has been to enable people unfamiliar with the field of sociology (and unlikely to be exposed to very much of it) to understand what is done in the field and why it is worthwhile. However, the book concentrates less on the field of sociology itself than on the sociologist and how he thinks about, observes, and analyzes the subject matter of his work.

I also hope this book answers at least some questions that students have about "relevance." It is sometimes difficult for teachers to understand why students do not intuitively perceive the relevance of their subjects to the world's work or its problems, but I think the request that relevance be explained is not at all unreasonable.

It seems to me that sociology has two points of decided relevance to the world and to the individual's life in it. It permits us to ask questions of the world, and therefore to derive answers, which no other form of inquiry can. In other words, it is aimed at a target whose relevance is only now beginning to be realized by college students. For all practical purposes, sociology and only sociology has as its central subject matter such phenomena as community power and decision-making, the impact of social class upon individual opportunities, the functions and consequences of racism and the means by which the interdependence of social institutions can form something like the so-called "military-industrial complex." Thus, some sociological comprehension is necessary in order to understand the world in which we live, to grasp what it is really like and what forces move and shape it. In today's world, the person ignorant of sociology (whether it is called by that name or not) is as incapable of understanding the forces that shape his destiny as is the person ignorant of science, mathematics, or even writing.

But sociology has a more personal relevance as well. For teaching purposes, I will advance the thesis in the following pages that man is socially determined—that he is a puppet, without choice and totally dependent upon and manipulated by the social forces which move him. This thesis is not really true, although I will maintain the position in order to explore how far it may be pushed in search of understanding. But it is too often true for too many people, for there *are* social forces to which we are all subjected and by which we are all shaped, whether we like it or not. Freedom consists in knowing what these forces are and how they work so that we have the option of saying no to the impact of their operation. For example, if we grow up in a racist society, we will be racists, unless we learn what racism is and how it works and then choose to refuse its impact. In order to do so, however, we must recognize that it is there in the first place. People often are puppets, blindly danced by strings of which they are unaware and over which they are not free to exercise control. A major function of sociology is that it permits us to recognize the forces operative on us and to untie the puppet strings which bind us, thereby giving us the option to be free.

The purpose of this book is not to "teach" sociology, and the student may well come away from it unable to recall the name of a single sociologist mentioned here. That doesn't matter; it is not the intent of the book. I make no claim to offer a general introduction to what sociology is all about or how the sociologist does his work or how the field came to be what it is today. There are texts and other readings for that purpose. This book is intended to permit an understanding of what we could call sociological perspective, a way of looking at the world which is peculiar to the discipline of sociology and which I think *is* sociology.

This book is not intended to stand alone. It is intended as a supplement to lectures and other classroom activities, to be used with a conventional text or with collections of paperbacks. A bibliography of paperbacks which I have found useful in introductory sociology classes may be found at the end of the book.

Acknowledgments

I must acknowledge gratefully, but with embarrassment, the work of many men and women who must go unnamed, persons whose ideas, and in some cases whose words, will appear on these pages without specific citation or acknowledgment. I know that much of what I write here is not my own, but it has come into my thoughts over the years from various sources and has lost specific identity. In a few instances I unquestionably admit that an idea or a sentence has come from someone else but that I cannot remember its origin. Therefore, to anyone recognizing his ideas or his words herein presented as my own, I offer my sincere apologies and my gratitude. No plagiarism is intended, and I would gladly acknowledge you if I could. I will certainly do so in any further edition if the matter is brought to my attention. In this sense, very little of this work is mine; most of the words may be original, but the ideas and argument are certainly derivative.

I wish also to express my gratitude to known persons who have made this work possible or who have had a hand in bringing it into being: to the students whose questions and interests have shaped by own during sixteen years of teaching introductory sociology at four different institutions; to Charlene S. Knuckman, whose prodding and editorial criticism of the early manuscript was invaluable; to Jackie Stringer for listening to and typing endless tapes; to Patra Noonan and Linda Lezark for secretarial services of high caliber; and to Joe Byers of The Dryden Press Inc. for being who he is.

Reece McGee
Purdue University
Spring 1972

Contents

Chapter 1

The Nature of Sociology

It is conventional to begin introductory books by defining the subject matter. Introductory sociology books are no exception to this convention. It may even be helpful to have the definitions, since what the student already "knows" may turn out to be incorrect. Nonetheless, sociologists who write such books often present only half-truths by giving overly brief definitions, such as: sociology is the study of human behavior, or of human social behavior, or of men in groups, and so on. Such definitions are too neat, telling little or nothing about sociology while appearing to tell everything. In fact, it is probably impossible to give a brief definition of the discipline which is reasonably accurate, since the field of sociology is too broad and too inclusive and has too many overlaps with other disciplines. The purpose of this book is to define sociology; the rest of this chapter is specifically devoted to such a definition.

Let us begin with the observation that there are two different kinds of approaches among the areas commonly called the social sciences. First, there are a number of specific social sciences—history, political science, economics, and so on—which deal with highly particular areas of human social behavior. Various aspects of these specific disciplines are frequently relevant to sociology. Second, in addition to these "focused" studies, there are also three general studies of man—anthropology, psychology, and sociology. These are called "general" because in one way or another they deal with the total behavior of man rather than with just a limited or particular facet. To a significant degree, the subject matter of the three is common to all of them. Although there are more useful ways of defining these areas, we will begin by noting the differences in subject matter which conventionally have served to distinguish one from another.

Traditional Distinctions among Anthropology, Psychology, and Sociology

Anthropology generally has concerned itself with studying total cultures of preliterate peoples. The anthropologist selects a particular culture in which he is interested and then tries to learn everything there is to know about it (in the same way that a marine biologist might attempt to make a total study of a form of marine life, including its life cycle, reproduction, food preferences, and so on). Thus, the anthropologist surveying an Indian tribe studies their language, economic system, kinship structure, marital practices, religion, daily routines, etc. He tries to gain a broad knowledge of the particular people and their way of life, frequently concentrating on behavior or customs which differ from those common to other cultures.

In the preceding paragraph the term *preliterate* was used to describe the kinds of societies anthropologists traditionally study. In other times such societies were often called primitive. For two reasons this usage is no longer considered appropriate in social science.

1.   It suggests that preliterate cultures are the ancestors of contemporary or "modern" ones, which they clearly are not; instead they are contemporary with many other cultures, including our own.

2.   This designation seems to connote some kind of superiority of the self-ordained "nonprimitive" world.

In English, at least, to call something primitive is to insult it, to suggest that it is uncivilized or, at best, untutored and immature. Stone Age cultures still exist, as do a number of other cultures without a form of writing. Most of these are primitive only in the sense that their technology is less well developed than ours. Technology, however, is only one among a host of criteria by which cultures may be judged. An H-bomb is the product of a more complex technology than is a stone ax. But the !Kung of the Kalihari Desert, for whom the ax is a prized possession, is, morally appalled by war as it is practiced by the Western world, and he regards its practitioners as bloodthirsty savages whose ways are incomprehensible to decent men. Who is to say that an ax-wielder with such ethics is more primitive than we "civilized" folk who kill each other by the tens of thousands?

The discipline of anthropology includes a number of subspecialities, such as physical anthropology (which is concerned with evolution and with determining and understanding the changing physical structure of the human being), linguistics, and archeology. But the traditional mainstream of the field has been cultural anthropology.

Psychology generally has been concerned with individuals rather than with total societies. The psychologist attempts to explain human behavior according to the particular characteristics of the actor. Thus, the psychologist studies learning, perception, memory, intelligence, and motivation in his attempt to learn why people behave as they do. Physiological phenomena, such as reflexes, are of interest to the psychologist because such physical characteristics help to form and to limit specific behavior. Individual attitudes and interests are investigated because they may account for motivation, the source of free-choice behavior. Clinical psychology, another area in the field, focuses on understanding and treating emotional and behavioral disorders of the types commonly referred to as neuroses and psychoses, or more generally as mental illness.

Sociology, as contrasted to the other two general social sciences, has concerned itself primarily with the study of human groups, including their effects on individual behavior in Western, literate societies. Although the sociologist has sometimes been accused of cultural bias for his focus on Western peoples, it is probably an inevitable preoccupation. The men who came to be known as anthropologists were at work chronicling the substance of preliterate cultures before the discipline of sociology evolved, and the few who chose to study in the emerging field of sociology were all from Western societies. (It should be noted, however, that the early European sociologists, who are considered the "fathers of sociology," were well aware of the importance of non-Western data and often used it in their researches.) In any event, the focus of sociology was early defined to consist not of whole societies but of social structures, social institutions, and social systems within given societies. Occasionally the focus was broadened to include comparisons of structures, institutions, and social systems across cultural boundaries (as in Max Weber's literary researches in religion).

Thus, the sociologist traditionally has included in his area of interest subunits of societies—groups, institutions, and varieties

of collective behavior displayed in churches, armies, bureauc-
racies, families, and so on. His general focus is on the behavior
of the groups themselves (for example, secret political organizations, ruling elites, and street corner gangs) and the effects
which membership in such specific groups may have on individuals. The kinds of questions a sociologist asks provide him
with answers which are the substance of sociology. He asks
questions such as the following:

> *What do the FBI, the NKVD, and the Gestapo have in com
> mon? From this information, what can we conclude is the
> nature and function of the secret police of Western societies?*

> *What appears to be the natural history of revolutionary polit-
> ical movements? Are there definable stages through which all
> or most political revolutions pass? What roles played by indi-
> vidual actors seem to be common among them?*

> *What characteristics do persons who share the same or simi-
> lar social roles have in common (be they alcoholics or social-
> ites, muggers or physicians)? Do their roles seem to have
> some purpose for the whole of society? Does the nature of
> this purpose, if discernible, influence the characteristics of
> those who play the roles, or are such characteristics learned
> in role-playing?*

In the nature and implications of traditionally sociological questions like these, we can begin to see that one aspect of the field
of sociology is its characteristic search for social causes of and
influences on human behavior. Thus, sociology is inescapably
bound up with some notion of *social determinism*—the belief
that society and social interactions among men cause, or at least
shape, human behavior.

We have described how the three fields—sociology, psychology, and anthropology—have traditionally been distinguished
from one another. But we also have suggested that much of the
subject matter of the three is common to all of them. Therefore, it may be more useful to introduce the discipline of soci-

ology by isolating the characteristics which are peculiar to it—its framework of explanation, its intellectual perspective, and its explanatory logic. These characteristics are visible in the ways in which sociologists ask questions and derive answers concerning subject matter that is shared with other social sciences. As indicated earlier, part of the framework of explanation is a strong interest in social determinism, but this is also shared with anthropology; part is an interest in or use of individual behavior as a subject of observation, but this is also shared with psychology. What is truly unique about sociology is the way in which it gives a specifically sociological meaning to subject matter, in other words, the way it interprets and applies its observations. This matter of interpretations, or assignment of meaning, constitutes the vital difference between fields in the social sciences.

The reader may wonder what is meant by the phrase *assignment of meaning*. He may ask how a sociological meaning can be imposed on subject matter which is common to other disciplines as well? After all, do not facts "speak for themselves"? Do they not exist "out there" in the world, awaiting human discovery? The answer is no. Facts do not have an unchanging meaning over time, they do not exist independent of human discovery, and they usually are not self-evident (as we imply when we say that they "speak for themselves"). Facts are given birth by men and given meaning by the context of their discovery, by men's understanding of and predisposition toward them. Facts do not exist in nature or in the world except for our understanding of them, and this understanding is a consequence of our rather highly selected perceptions of and agreements about them. Thus, "fact" and the "truth" which is based upon it are relative to human knowledge, understanding, interpretation, and perception. These human elements along with related collections of "fact" provide the context in which any particular fact is evaluated or permitted to speak for itself.

But perhaps an example would be more effective in making this point. If it is known that there exists in the United States an area in which 38 percent of the family residences have running water, what is the meaning of this fact? By itself, it has very little meaning. But if we add to that information the additional information that the area consists of several square blocks on Manhattan Island, it is possible to conclude that the area in question must be one of the most deprived slums in the country. If, on the other hand, we are informed that the area in question is located in Alaska and is an entire county, the meaning of the fact is quite different. That county may be one of the major urban areas of the state, since Alaska is the most sparsely inhabited state of the union; and while sparseness is not the determining factor, it is an indicator of the stage of development of the area being considered. Specifically, household running water is available in New York City, but such a stage of technology cannot be assumed for an Alaskan community. Thus, the meaning of the 38 percent does not lie in the fact itself but in the total context of its interpretation by men. Meaning is imposed on the fact by men, by their understanding of the frame of reference for that fact. Meaning, then, is not something discovered "out there" in the world; instead it is a product of human effort that is given to the world.

We are accustomed to thinking of ourselves as inhabiting an orderly universe, one regulated by natural or scientific laws. Yet this notion, too, reveals a lack of understanding of the nature of knowledge. The laws of science are man-made, invented generalities. They are an attempt to describe an order which man perceives in the universe. A simple statement of the logic of scientific law is: If we look at the world in a certain way, then we are very likely to see the following kinds of things. Of course, there must be things to be seen; but what those things are, how they operate, and whether they are orderly or regular is a consequence of the seeing process, not necessarily of the nature of the things themselves. What we perceive to be the nature of things is a result of what we are looking for and which aspects we choose to emphasize or ignore. Consider, for example, a St. Bernard and a Chihuahua, standing side by side. If we were asked to tell why they are alike, we probably would begin by noting that both are dogs. But is the "doggishness" which we see in both of them a consequence of something truly alike in these animals, or is it the result of using the category "dog" which we knew beforehand was common to them both?

If we had never seen a dog (except perhaps in books and magazines), would we have recognized either animal as being a dog? More particularly, would we have recognized both as being dogs? For, are they not really most unlike to the unfamiliar eye? Certainly, they share biological similarities, which is why we classify both as dogs. But in the case of these two breeds the similarities are less immediately visible to the naked eye than are the differences, which are much more evident and enormous. We classify them as alike only by the less than self-evident biological characteristics which they share. If we had used as criteria the more visible characteristics of the two (size, weight, amount of hair, and so on), we would consider them to be very dissimilar creatures. But we are used to classifying animals according to conventional characteristics which we have learned. Therefore, we tend to perceive such qualities as a constant rather than a standard classificatory scheme which could be changed by common agreement. Thus, the "order in the universe" which allows both Chihuahuas and St. Bernards to be dogs lies not in that universe but rather in an agreement on classification scheme.

The various parts which make up this or any classification scheme, although man-made, do refer to concrete phenomena in the world. What is arbitrary is the selection of any particular set of phenomena, or facts, to serve as the basis for a system of classification. So the "order" which we find in the universe is not actually there at all, unless the human classification scheme which created it is also there. The "ultimate reality" of the universe is probably chaos; we put it in order by using our perceptions and rules and by creating symbols that allow those perceptions to have reasonable or sensible "meanings." The function of the various intellectual pursuits is to provide us with the meanings which we use to see, order, describe, study, and change our world.

Truth in the world is based on observed facts. But if the meanings of such facts are relative to their contexts, and if these contexts are but convenient classifying inventions of man, then truth must be relative and variable. This is unlike the "truth" of an ethical or aesthetic system, which is based on belief rather than observation of facts. Thus, for it to be "wrong to kill" is "true" within the limits described by the Judeo-Christian conception of murder; however, this statement of belief does not describe anything about the way the world is observed to work. The failure to distinguish between these two meanings for the word *truth* is responsible for a great deal of semantic and political confusion.

If scientific truth is based on a commonly agreed upon set of observations, then truth becomes a function of observation and must be based on what is selected for attention, what is taken for granted, and what is selected for logical classification. As a consequence, the scientist must accustom himself to living with alternative truths produced by alternative sets of observations. The history of the physical sciences is full of such examples. The "truths" of the mutually contradictory theories of light (wave versus corpuscular) are probably classic. Light observed one way behaves as if it were being transmitted in the form of a continuous wave. Observed another way, it appears as if it were being transmitted in the form of individual particles. Since both explanations of the nature of light are necessary to adequately describe its observed behavior, both are accepted as true even though they contradict one another.

Explanations must be fitted to observation and accepted as true on the basis of what is being observed and why. The physicist wanting to do one kind of experiment adopts the explanation of light which is most consistent with what he is trying to accomplish; he used the "truth" which fits best. So truth, like fact, is a variable rather than a constant, even though we are accustomed to thinking of them both as unchanging.

In certain aspects of our lives we are comfortable with such variables and do not find them perplexing. No one would be surprised if a carpenter and a nuclear physicist gave different explanations about the structure of a chair. Since each man explains things within the framework of his occupation, the explanations will be radically different. The person asking about the chair's structure will have to select the most appropriate answer, depending upon what he wants to do with the explanation. In this sense, truth is a function of the questions asked and the reasons for asking them in the first place. It is always tentative, and it is always pragmatic.

This observation about truth brings us back again to the nature of sociology and the distinctions between it and the other social sciences. Earlier in this chapter we mentioned that while it had been traditional to differentiate the social sciences according to subject matter, it is probably more useful to differentiate them according to the ways by which they give meaning to their observations. The most common denominator of social behavior, whether studied by the sociologist, psychologist, or anthropologist, is some action of a human being involved either directly or indirectly with other people. Eating with a fork or with chopsticks is a social action; eating as a biological need is not. Wearing a tie, waving at a friend, driving on the right side of the street, and styling one's hair are social actions. All of them can be directly observed, cannot be broken apart into smaller directly observed parts, and can be selected for study by a student of any of the three social sciences. Yet, the explanations offered for any of these actions by a sociologist, a psychologist, or an anthropologist would be different, since each of the three organizes his observations and meanings differently. Each one uses what can be called an alternative framework of explanation.

Sociology is characterized by a framework of explanation that attempts to describe and explain human behavior as a consequence of the characteristics of the social groups to which people belong. Usually, but not necessarily, this framework applies to explanations made for industrialized societies. So a sociological explanation for events or phenomena is simply one that interprets them in terms of the influence which a group has on its members. In this sense, sociology can be said to involve social determinism, since the purpose of the field is to view human hehavior as a consequence of collective social influences. Is this the only possible explanation for the events of our world? Of course not, but such an explanation is the singular function of sociology. If others are adopted, then they are by definition not sociological; instead they are psychological or chemical or physiological or theological, to name only a few of the possible alternative frameworks of explanation.

Such differing frameworks can be viewed as *constitutive rules*—rules that are used in defining an enterprise or activity. In the case of sociology, they are rules used for interpreting observed aspects of human behavior. An analogy with games is both useful and inescapable. Games are defined, organized, and constituted by rules. The rules tell the object of the game, the limits within which it is to be played, and the exact ways in which it is to be played; they explain the nature and use of the equipment involved and provide the definition of winning and losing. In order to play a particular game, the rules of that game must be followed. For example, someone could invent a variety of games utilizing checkers and a checkerboard, but only one game would be checkers according to the commonly accepted rules of that game. The others would all be different games. In the same way that rules describe the ways of assigning meaning to games, they also define, characterize, and differentiate the various intellectual enterprises. In fact, this is what the different intellectual enterprises are all about: interpreting and assigning meaning to the world according to a particular set of rules.

For sociology, the constitutive rules involve the use of various aspects of group phenomena to give order to the infinite and chaotic possibilities of observed human behavior. Thus, when we observe that throughout the world the suicide rate among Roman Catholics is lower than it is among members of other Christian religions, we look for an explanation not in some physiological peculiarity of Catholics, not in some quirk of their psychology, but rather in the characteristics of the group to which all Catholics belong. In so doing, we discover that self-murder is more strongly condemned by that Christian denomination than by the others and that Catholics as a group tend to experience a greater sense of solidarity with their religious organization than do most other Christians; this results in greater support of their religion's customs and beliefs. A psychologist could take the same initial information and come up with an entirely different explanation. However, since we have framed our explanation in terms of the characteristics of a social group, our explanation is a sociological one.

Sociological Thinking

The above example suggests again that one aspect of sociological thinking which makes the field unique among other disciplines is the way it assigns meaning—its *constitutive rules for explanation*. A second unique characteristic of sociology is its *probabilistic thinking*. This kind of thinking involves a consideration of events in terms of their relationship to other events which seem to have been their cause or their outcome. Probabilistic types of thinking are used in sociology because pure cause-and-effect relationships in human social behavior are extremely difficult to establish. In fact, often they do not seem to operate at all, at least in the sense that they can be demonstrated like the laws of physical science. Therefore, rather than deal with cause-and-effect, sociologist prefers to discover and assess the association of things. Certain kinds of events seem to be associated with each other in certain ways under certain circumstances. Thus, there is a probability that such events will be associated with each other in any specific case. For example, a certain suicide rate is associated with one religious population, while a different suicide rate is associated with another. In the example discussed earlier, being Catholic neither *prevents* an individual from committing suicide nor *causes* him to reject this type of behavior. But there is a measurable probability that any given Catholic is less likely to commit suicide than any given Protestant.

Obviously, the possibility of computing probability depends upon the possession of accurate observations, or data, concerning the events being studied. In order to make probability statements about any aspect of the world, we must first have a body of reasonably accurate information concerning it. The information also must be expressed (or be capable of being expressed) in a quantitative or numerical form. Many qualitative or metaphysical propositions are eliminated from sociological study because they are incapable of being translated to numerical probabilities. This means that much of the logic of sociological thought will be *inductive*—a logic of inference, which moves from specific observations to generalizations. The sociologist must collect enough specific observations so that he can ultimately feel secure in making a leap from a description of each item observed to a generalizing statement about all of them. For example, a sociologist might observe the following: Male number one is larger than female number one, male number two is larger than female number two, and so on. The sociologist would continue his observations until he felt confident enough to say that in general men are larger than women, even though he had not looked at all men and all women. The vital point in inference logic is that the observer draws his conclusions without looking at the total available sample of what he is observing.

The dependence upon inductive reasoning in sociology involves a further use of probabilistic thinking. No matter how accurate the observations upon which one's generalizations are based, if they do not include every example of the behavior observed, the generalization may be proved wrong when applied to another case in question. Thus, probabilistic thinking (or inductive reasoning) as it is practiced in sociology may be thought of as a logic of statistical inference. The sociologist is caught up in a constantly recurring dilemma. Even when he knows the characteristics of the subject under study (and usually he doesn't), he rarely has total knowledge of it. So his conclusions are at best guesses based on some computable probability. But he is never sure of his conclusions and never can be. The generalization (prediction) he makes, although based on the best and most carefully described data available to him, may prove to be wrong either because the characteristics of his subject were more varied than he knew or because his sampling, just by the luck of the draw, proved to be inaccurate.

For these reasons, sociological generalizations are usually stated in a probabilistic fashion: Persons with incomes below X thousand dollars a year *are likely* to vote Democratic in national elections, if they vote at all; Catholics *tend to* commit suicide less frequently than Protestants; there is a *higher incidence* of alcoholism among house painters than among medical technicians. From such statements, it is possible to estimate the likelihood of a particular house painter being an alcoholic or of a particular Protestant committing suicide, assuming all the while that such persons are typical examples within their category. Sometimes, knowledge of the characteristics of a particular category permits an explanation of the association between the category and the behavior in question (as, for example, in the earlier discussion of the lower suicide rate among Catholics).

Besides the logic of induction, based on factual knowledge, there is the logic of deduction, based on formal knowledge—knowledge obtained from the application of the rules of formal systems such as mathematics or grammar to a body of data. Deductive logic is based on rules rather than observations and generalizations about the world. For example: "All uncles are male" sounds like a statement of fact, but upon examination it turns out to be a description created by one of the rules of usage in the English language. Uncles are male *by definition*. One does not need to observe a quantity of uncles to discover that they are always men; one need only understand the English language. It is a matter of logically applying the rules. If the rules for the use of English are properly observed, the word *uncle* will never be applied to a female.

Formal knowledge is found principally in scientific theory, where logic becomes a critical part of theory construction. Its chief use is in the deduction of hypotheses from a general statement of circumstances. Deduction is the process of working from general to particular statements. (Assume that all crows are black. If someone is going to show me his pet crow, I will expect that crow to be black, too.) Beginning students will rarely encounter formal knowledge systems in sociology, for the significance of formal theory in the field is small, compared to its significance in other fields.

Suggested for Further Reading

Peter Berger, *Invitation to Sociology*
William Bruce Cameron, *Informal Sociology*
Hinkle and Hinkle, *Development of Modern Sociology*
C. Wright Mills, *White Collar*
Eugene Webb, et al., *Unobtrusive Measures*

Topics and Questions for Discussion

1. A Martian sociologist proposes to do a study of U.S. cultural values. His method will be to study in depth one U.S. citizen selected at random. His justification for this methodology is that he is short of both funds and time and, being exposed to the same culture, all Americans may be considered as being alike since they are identical except for obvious physical differences in sex, size, and color. What types of problems of interpretation is he building into his research? Why?

2. Since cultures place distinctive marks on the human personality by means of socialization and since the socialization processes vary among different subcultures and/or geographic areas, we would expect each different culture to produce its own "basic personality" type. What are some of the dangers in immediately assuming that an individual is representing such a "basic personality?"

3. In what way does the concept of culture help us to understand reality? And what is the relationship between reality and cultural rules?

Chapter 2

Culture: The Most Fundamental Idea

Definitions and Use

The concept of culture is fundamental in sociology and anthropology. Indeed, it is so important that it can be regarded as being the single most useful idea we have for understanding and ordering the phenomena we observe. It is used by social scientists in several related ways which can be easily distinguished from one another by context once one is familiar with the term.

The general definition of culture which this book will follow is that offered by one of the deans of American anthropology, Clyde Kluckhohn. He defines culture as an historically derived system of explicit and implicit designs for living which tend to be shared by all or specifically designated members of a group or a society.[1] While all the qualifying phrases in this definition are useful in one way or another, the really important one is *explicit and implicit designs for living.* Culture, then, refers to ways of behaving or doing things, patterns of behavior for the members of a society. It is not the actual behaving or doing of things but the ways in which those things are done. Some of them are overt and explicit, and some are hidden and implicit.

Every human society, however large or small, can be said to have a culture of its own, or ways of doing things which to some extent are peculiar to it and mark it off from other societies. (If this were not so, it would be impossible to distinguish one society from another, because the behavior of their members would be identical.) But the word *culture* also refers to behavior characterizing groups of people which are both larger and smaller than specific societies.[2] The example of the Plains

---

[1] Clyde Kluckhohn and William Kelly, "The Concept of Culture," *The Science of Man in the World Crisis*, ed. Ralph Linton (New York: Columbia University Press, 1945), p. 97.

[2] The words *culture* and *society* are sometimes used interchangeably by social scientists; their meaning is usually discernible by context. To the extent that we may wish to differentiate them, however, we may adopt the definition of culture already given and regard society as referring to an identifiable group of people inhabiting a geographically definable territory and possessing a culture of their own which distinguishes them from other similar groups. A society *is not the same thing* as a nation-

Indians of the United States can be used to explain some of the different ways in which the term *culture* is commonly used.[3] At the time of their conquest, there lived in that area of the United States known as the Great Plains no fewer than thirty-one Amerind (American Indian) societies, each with its own name, culture, and language. Taken as a whole, each society (tribe) was different from any one of the other thirty societies, and all were politically independent. But all the tribes also had a great deal of behavior in common, including the following: All thirty-one tribes hunted buffalo as their food staple, made their dwellings (teepees) of poles and skin and usually set them up in a camp circle, made clothing of buffalo and deer hide and also used the hides for many other purposes, created geometric art works, organized men into warrior clubs where they earned status through combative prowess, and practiced the sun dance. These common ways of behaving among the thirty-one tribes are what anthropologists call "Plains Indian culture." *Plains culture* is a term used to distinguish these Indians and their common behavior from other Indians with different shared behaviors (as, for example, the Eastern Woodland culture, to which the famous Iroquois Confederacy would belong, or the Pueblo culture, to which the Navajo and Hopi would belong). In this sense, the word *culture* refers to ways of behaving which are shared by a group larger than any given specific society.

Culture can also refer to behavior which characterizes human subgroups within specific societies. When used this way the word is usually modified into *subculture*. There are occupational subcultures, for example, which distinguish military, medical, or railroad families from other people in the same society; ethnic or racial subcultures among native-born American blacks, Italians, or Mexican—Americans; illegal subcultures

---

state, although the two *may be the same*. (The Soviet Union, for example, encompasses a number of different societies and cultures.) Some cultures can exist without the physical presence of societies to sustain them.

[3]   Ralph L. Beals and Harry Hoijer, *An Introduction to Anthropology* (3rd ed.; New York: The Macmillan Company, 1965), pp. 267-68.

of crime and politics, and so on. In the United States all native-born physicians share in the general American culture into which they were born, but they also share other behavior traits only with each other (for example, language usages, work duties, and attitudes toward certain events). These traits are acquired as a result of a long period of occupational preparation and therefore are not characteristic of other Americans (although some of the traits might occur among dentists, medical technicians, or nurses, who are also associated with the health service professions).

The term *culture* is used sometimes to refer to all human behavior throughout history (as in the phrase *human culture*), to ways of behaving that are common to all or most men at any one period in history (Stone Age culture), or to ways of behaving common to groups of societies in particular historical epochs. Thus, the "culture of the High Middle Ages" implicitly excludes non-European societies, and "twentieth century culture" implicitly excludes preliterate societies and developing nations.

As we said earlier, the many uses of the word *culture* can be distinguished from each other by the context in which they appear. However, the meaning we shall adhere to in this book is that culture is a pattern of behavior for members of a particular society.

Culture Is Learned

The definition of *culture* as "designs for living" implies that it is learned. Culture is not inherited genetically like eye color or stature, and cultural behavior is not something we "just naturally" do in some more or less instincitive way. Therefore, when we talk about culture or cultural phenomena, we are talking about learned behavior. Not all human behavior is learned. Sneezing, swallowing, and blinking are essentially physiological; they are simply the way in which the organic mechanism of the body works. Other behavior could be called genetic, in that it is the consequence of the peculiarly *human* construction of our bodies (for example, three-dimensional vision, upright carriage, and opposable thumbs, and the behaviors determined or made possible by such physical features). But as a general rule, the sociologist is normally interested only in those behaviors which are either entirely cultural or else so strongly influenced by cultural phenomena as to not have a significant physiological or genetic basis. Such behaviors as these are learned.

The popular belief in "human instinct," "basic instinct," or "human nature," in the sense of behaviors which are natural to all human beings because they are human, has no basis in fact. Human beings do not have instincts in the way that other animals do. In biology, the word *instinct* refers to a constant and complicated inherited (genetically-transmitted) behavior which is unchangeable by the animal. Familiar examples are nest-building in birds, the return of salmon to their home streams to spawn, and direction-finding in many species. The importance of truly instinctive animal behavior is that it is not learned by the individual. It is not taught to him by his mother. Even if he is raised in utter isolation from all others of his kind, at the appropriate point in his life cycle, if permitted to do so, the individual animal will engage in the behavior in question in exactly the same way that all others of his kind do. It is not something he has a choice about and not something he can elect to do in a particular manner. It is as "biological" as breathing; and, as with breathing, the animal is not even aware of what he is doing.

Human beings do not engage in behavior of this kind. We are born with *reflexes*, such as pupillary contraction and the knee-jerk, which are inherited and not variable by any act of will of the individual. But these are not the complex behaviors that the word *instinct* refers to when applied to animals; no complex human behavior is invariant. If, for example, there were an instinct for self-preservation (a popular conception), suicide would be impossible, because the nature of our genetic structure would not permit it. Similarly, if there were instincts for courage or mother love, cowardice and infanticide would be unknown. Indeed, what many people think of as being instinctive or as resulting from "human nature" often is simply whatever is commonly accepted as being "natural" in that culture, that is, the way things with which they are familiar are usually done. That it is only "human nature" to take an offered advantage, to covet property, and to be suspicious of a person with a different skin color are all familiar misconceptions growing out of cultural phenomena. Something cannot be "just human nature" where even one negative case occurs.

Learned cultural phenomena are of major significance for our behavior, because this kind of acculturation (acquisition of cultural characteristics) can be so powerful that it is actually capable of modifying physiologically-based behaviors. We cannot by an act of will, change our pupillary reflexes, but a fairly simple psychological procedure called conditioning can do so quite readily. Indeed, such conditioning can induce reflexive behavior to occur upon the presentation of a stimulus, such as a ringing bell, which has no organic connection with the reflex that is then exhibited. Similarly, many Americans regard it as natural that the physiological behavior of excretion should be trained (regulated) in infants as young as six months of age; but they would be amazed to see Polynesian children of the same age swimming by themselves in the ocean. Both examples involve a social or cultural modification of biologically-based behavior. What makes them particularly interesting is that our amazement can be reversed, because Polynesian adults regard it as biologically impossible for children to be toilet-trained before they can speak.

Therefore, the importance of genetic or physiological structure to our behavior is not in what it makes us do. There appear to be few genetic determinants of human activity, but there are, unquestionably, genetically or physiologically imposed *limitations* upon what is possible for us to do. We are not forced by our genetic nature to be hostile to another person simply because his skin is of a different color, but neither is there anything about our genetic makeup which forbids such behavior. The structure of our forearms determines that we will not fly by waving our arms, but it does not force us to use those arms to play baseball or to drive an automobile. Thus, our bodies and our biological heritage impose limits upon what we as humans are able to do, but they only rarely impose particular behaviors upon us.[4]

However, culture does impose particular behaviors on us. That is, we learn to behave in accordance with the expectations of the culture (or cultures) in which we are raised. Culture itself is an abstraction from behavior, an inference based upon observations of persons behaving; it is the way in which something is commonly made or done or used. We cannot observe culture directly, but as we observe things and people, we find regularities from which we may infer the existence of a culture pattern. To illustrate, if someone from a tropical island were visiting North America for the first time, he would notice that men almost invariably wear what we call trousers. (While women wear these garments sometimes, they also show a greater variety in their choice of wearing apparel.) Observing the regularity with which such garments are associated with men, the islander would have to conclude either that this regularity was accidental (it just happened that wherever he went the only men he saw were wearing trousers) or that some pattern directed the behavior. If he chose the latter explanation, he would infer the existence of a culture item prescribing trousers as an appropriate garment for men.

In this simple example we have not observed the culture. We have seen that men wear trousers, and from the regularity of this behavior we have inferred (or abstracted) the existence in North American culture of a custom for male attire. Thus, we never observe the custom itself; we only observe people be-

---

[4]   Of possible relevance, however, is Robert Ardrey's argument, developed in *African Genesis* (New York: Dell Publishing Company, Inc., 1961) and other works, concerning man's essentially primate and anthropoid nature. Ardrey believes that this nature may impose some instinctive or quasi-instinctive behaviors upon man (for example, territoriality—defining some territory or space as "private property"). In *African Genesis*, he argues that the use of tools—specifically, weapons—may have permitted man to evolve from an anthropoid state, rather than that evolution permitted the eventual use of tools. If true, this argument would imply that human ferocity and aggressiveness are instinctive, although even so, it would not demand that we express them in the form of modern warfare. The evidence at this point is insufficient to make this more than an interesting, and evocative, speculation.

having in accord with it. Our conclusion is that they behave that way because of the existence of such a custom. In a sense, we could say that culture is discovered by the observer, whether he is a participant or an outsider with a social science orientation.

We conclude from this discussion that culture is real, even though it does not have a specific physical location. We see that it exists, that people respond to it, and that we can see them performing culturally acquired actions. However, since it is an abstraction, it can be known (or discovered) only by inference, as a conclusion based upon observation of human behavior. While some culture items are material things (for example, automobiles, crossbows, and tobacco pouches), the cultural definitions and meanings of them and the rules for their use are nonmaterial. But as the definition of culture implies, the designs for living which Kluckhohn speaks of—those rules defining, demanding, and restricting our behavior—are probably far more important than material cultural items in understanding human behavior. These cultural rules are called *norms*. Some norms are explicit and open, known to the participants in a culture. Traffic regulations (and all other laws) are an example of such explicit norms; the wearing of trousers by North American men is probably another. But many norms are implicit and hidden; they are not specifically known or recognized by members of the culture where they are found, even though the people respond to them and act them out every day of their lives. An illustration of these implicit norms involves the culturally determined rules for the use of space between people. Those of us who are North Americans have never been specifically instructed in the rules for the appropriate distance to keep from other people while talking with them. But we all know and practice the rules, even though such rules are complicated, dictated by social status and by our relationship with the person with whom we are talking. For example, we all recognize that it would be inappropriate for a man to carry on an intimate conversation with his fiancee from a distance of forty inches (literally "arm's length") and that it would be equally inappropriate for someone to speak with a recently-introduced person of the opposite sex from a distance of four inches. It is quite all right to put one's face up close to talk to a three-year-old child whom one has just met, regardless of the child's sex, while it would be a very rude thing to do with a just-introduced seventy-year-old person.[5] The fact that we recognize these examples demonstrates the existence of cultural norms defining the use of space, but we do not know what these rules are. That is, although we act them out, we are not aware of them as rules to which we must respond. Only when their existence as rules is pointed out to us do we begin to formulate questions which will permit us to observe our behavior or that of other people in order to infer what these rules are. Thus, as we pointed out earlier, many cultural norms are implicit, consciously unknown to the members of the society possessing them. A major task of sociology is that of clearly explaining the implicit cultural norms of our social life.

Culture and Norms

The preceding discussion should have begun to make clear that culture is the product of norms as well as their source. One of the ways in which we discover the nature of a given culture is by watching what people do and inferring the existence of norms from the regularities we find in their behavior. In this sense, the regularity of behavior is attributable to the existence of a norm; and when we have discovered the central norms of a society through observation of its regularities, we have learned something of its culture. Thus, culture, as defined by the process of studying it, is a product of the norms of a society as well as their source. One way of understanding culture, then, is to regard it as consisting centrally of norms, while those same norms are simultaneously regarded as products of the culture in which they occur. If this seems confusing, perhaps a question-and-answer format will help to clarify the relationship of the concepts.

---

[5]   The study of the social uses of space is called proxemics in anthropology, and it is one of that field's fastest growing subspecialities. See Edward T. Hall, *The Silent Language* (New York: Doubleday & Company, Inc., 1959) and O. Michael Watson, *Proxemic Behavior: A Cross-Cultural Study* (The Hague: Mouton, 1970).

What is culture? Patterns for behavior or designs for living inferred from observed regularities in social behavior.

What accounts for such regularities? That people respond to specific rules or norms about how to behave and about the meanings of things.

Where do these rules or norms originate? In the culture.

Another way of getting at the same general idea would be to say that in several very important senses culture *is* norms and norms *are* culture.

We should also understand that culture is man's most important survival mechanism. Man lacks instincts, which are nature's way of assisting many other animals to survive by forcing them to behave in protective ways. Man also lacks the powerful muscles, teeth, and speed that enable other animals to survive. Instead of these, man has survived and conquered in the world through the medium of culture. Man does not have thick fur with which to withstand the winter cold, but long before the dawn of written history he learned to make fire and wear skins of other animals, thus accomplishing the same purpose. He does not have the claws of the great cats or the strength of the bear, but before man came out of his caves he had learned to throw sharpened stones and had begun to hunt those animals as prey. It is interesting to speculate upon the probability that in the anthropoidal, prehuman evolutionary stages, the creatures that were the ancestors of men were undoubtedly more hunted than hunters. And while our bodies have changed considerably since that time, they are probably even less adapted to "fight or flight" than were those of our forefathers. What has enabled men to conquer the earth, and either enslave or exterminate other life forms on it, has been his acquired culture. Once men became socially organized and began working together (which probably presumes some power of speech), and once they learned to use the simplest tool (the hand ax), their future on this planet was assured.

We can see the utility of our culture as a survival mechanism in the phenomenon known as *cultural persistence*—the fact that when inventions, ideas, and discoveries become a part of the cultural mainstream, they remain there even over very long periods of time. Many of the preliterate peoples of the world still use as everyday artifacts tools invented by Stone Age man. And while we North Americans do not use them every day, we retain in our urbanized, industrialized, highly mechanized culture much of the knowledge and skill passed on by these distant ancestors. For example, most of us know that we can harden the point of a wooden spear by baking or charring it in a fire. This is one of the fundamental human discoveries of all time, one which may be almost two million years old; yet, it persists as knowledge in American culture today. Similarly, if we were faced with the problem of producing fire without matches or flint and steel, we would probably remember that we had somehow heard of an ancient technique utilizing a bow-drill (a wooden stick or drill which is turned in a pile of flammable material by wrapping a turn or two of bowstring about it and then sawing with the bow to produce heat through friction). Culture, then, tends to persist, and this persistence contributes to its capacity to aid human survival. There are no lost arts.[6]

We said earlier that culture *is* norms, but since norms are also the products of a culture, the question of their origin needs a fuller answer. Where do norms come from in the first place? How are they invented and adopted? Kluckhohn speaks of culture as being historically derived designs for living. Norms, then, are the products of a people's history; they are the ways people, by the experience of living, solve the problems which life pre-

[6] This is not to say that nothing is ever "forgotten by history." To use the example that students frequently mention, we cannot duplicate exactly the embalming techniques of ancient Egypt or the stained glass of the medieval cathedral. But it is unnecessary that we do so. Modern techniques for preservation of organic materials and for coloring glass are much superior to ancient ones; thus, the practices have not only not been lost, they have been improved upon. And the marvelously lustrous colors of medieval stained glass are the product of unknown imperfections in the ancient glass, not a lost secret of the glassmakers.

sents. Some norms are deliberately invented in order to deal with particular problems. Laws are an example of norms of this type; as new discoveries or experiences present new problems, we create legal rules as a means of dealing with them. Other norms apparently "just happen"; methods of dealing with or defining phenomena or of doing things in certain ways become normative through acceptance and repetition. An example of this kind of norm is the practice in most families of having everyone sit in a particular place at the dinner table; the family members (particularly the small children) become distinctly uncomfortable when these seating rules are violated. That such usages are normative is explicitly recognized in the child's com plaint (or that of the Three Bears): "Someone's been sitting in *my* chair!"

Thus, norms develop because they are functional (useful) for the society in which they occur. The simple process of living presents problems which have to be solved, and when it becomes customary to do something in a particular way, societies often make that way of doing it preferential or mandatory by defining it as proper. Men must find wives and women husbands, children must be named, crops planted, and so on; norms arise as locally preferred solutions to such problems. Certain categories of life problems, such as the production of goods or the maintenance of social order, are sometimes called "functional imperatives" of human society, since they represent phenomena with which every society must deal in order to endure. The norm systems which each culture develops or adopts can be viewed as responses to these requirements.

It should go without saying that since these common life problems may be solved in a variety of different ways, different societies will work out different ways of handling them. The fact that a given problem must be solved does not in any way determine how that task should be carried out. Thus, what is deemed the only right and proper way for something to be done in one society may be regarded as an abomination in another. The understanding of this phenomenon is called "cultural relativity"; its converse is called "ethnocentrism" and involves the belief that one's own ways of doing things are the only right, proper, just, and moral ways. Ethnocentrism is a common human phenomenon that has resulted in some of our most hideous behaviors, including war, racism, and genocide. The solution to it is a recognition of the common humanity of all men and of the diversity of other normative systems as simply reflecting their differing historical experiences.

Varieties of Norms

We said earlier that norms can be viewed as a society's methods for meeting life's problems. Some of these are simply customary, the way things happened to work out, while some are explicitly invented and required in order to accomplish a specifically perceived purpose. Norms, then, come in a variety of forms and are implemented in different ways. One way of distinguishing among them is to classify them as being either *folkways* or *mores* according to a set of distinctions originated by the sociologist William Graham Sumner in the early 1900s. Sumner taught that folkways are norms, habitual ways of behaving the arise out of the adjustment of people to other people and to places; in other words, folkways are customary behaviors arising out of everyday interactions. According to Sumner, the distinguishing property of folkways is not in their genesis but in the manner in which people react when they are violated.[7] The violation of a folkway is noticed by other people and is disturbing to them, but they do not feel required to punish the violator. Mores also are norms, but their violation arouses strong feelings in the onlooker, who may feel compelled to punish the violator himself or to insure that he is punished. We distinguish between the two kinds of norms not according to their content (because norms can be about anything) but according to the social reaction which their violation receives. This implies that if we are strangers to a culture, we will be unable to predict ahead of time what phenomena will be regarded as important, or even sacred, and what will be considered trivial. There are probably no behaviors which all societies regard as important in the same ways.

---

[7]   William Graham Sumner, *Folkways* (New York: Dover Publications, Inc., 1906), Chapter 1.

Another way to think of the distinction between folkways and mores is to regard the word *folkways* as being synonymous with *customs* and the word *mores* as synonymous with *morals*. Mores are customs which a given society values so much that conformity with them is widely accepted as being important to the society itself; thus, failure to observe them is disturbing to others and will be reacted to by them Folkways are simply the ways in which things are usually done, and while others may notice if they are not followed, it is not considered improper not to do so. Ideas of propriety, then, distinguish the mores of a society.

Another norm concept common to the social sciences is that of the *taboo*. Taboos may be thought of as a special class of mores, distinguished from other mores as being behaviors which are defined in the concerned society as too loathsome, abhorrent, or terrible for anyone in the society to contemplate. Taboos may prohibit behavior which is considered so obscene or revolting that the society has never bothered to enact laws against it. In the United States, cannibalism would be an example of tabooed behavior. Despite an American penchant for trying to regulate customary behavior through law, many of the fifty states have not felt it necessary to make the practice of cannibalism illegal. Nor are Americans threatened with inundation by cannibals as a result of this fact. Because the practice is so widely tabooed, not just in the United States but throughout most of the civilized world, laws specifically forbidding it are unnecessary. In preliterate societies, taboo violation is likely to be defined as an offense against the gods, and punishment (aside from the ostracism imposed by peoples' abhorrence) may be left up to them. In the United States, we are likely to define a taboo violator as insane and clap him into a mental hospital (on the grounds that anyone who behaved in such a revolting a manner could not be of sound mind). As in the case of other mores, anything can be tabooed in a given society, and anthropology and history show that the behaviors which have been tabooed from time to time in one place or another are quite varied. Probably the most common taboos are against incest (although what constitutes such behavior is variously defined), cannibalism, and assorted foodstuffs.

The last variety of norm which we will discuss is *law.* Laws differ from other kinds of norms in several important ways. Laws are specifically and consciously enacted for some purpose, while folkways and mores "just happen" (although many societies enact into laws some of their folkways and mores, which somewhat confuses the matter). Laws are also different from other norms in that they may or may not deal with matters about which people have sentiments, and their violation may or may not be sanctioned by the public at large. Indeed, sometimes laws are so unpopular that their violation is supported by public sentiment. Tax laws often bring out these feelings, but few of us have our passions aroused by laws providing for the nautral fiber content of mattresses. Laws differ from the customary norms in other ways as well. One important difference is that what constitutes a violation of law is always specifically stated, while folkways and more are often extremely ambiguous regarding violation. Laws also state exactly what that punishment for a given violation is ("not more than three nor less than one year and a fine not to exceed . . . ") Finally, laws are enforced by specific organs of government (the courts and police, a warrior group, a council of old women, and so on). While we North Americans tend to think of law as consisting of the apparatus of courts and police and, above all, written documents, it is in fact found in all societies preliterate as well as literate, and may be carried on just as well by oral tradition as by law books.[8]

Norms and Compulsion

The discussion of varieties of norms was opened with the observation that reactions to norm violations are what enables us to distinguish among the various norms. We can classify norms by positioning them on a continuum of compulsion, distinguished from one another by the amount of compulsion a society imposes upon its members to secure normative conformity. Using this classification scheme, we can visualize in the sketch below the types of norms we have been discussing.

---

[8]   See E. A. Hoebel, *The Law of Primitive Man: A Study in Comparative Legal Dynamics* (Cambridge: Harvard University Press, 1964).

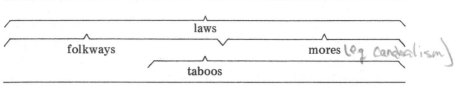

no compulsion   ultimate compulsion

Since we are talking about classes of norms, none of the varieties occupies a single point on the continuum; instead, all norms are enforced by ranges of compulsion, depending upon the specific behavior in question. In some cases the ranges overlap. Also, what constitutes "ultimate compulsion" is not defined in the diagram, for the extent of a sanction is culturally variable. In some societies, execution or expulsion from the group may constitute the worst punishment for a norm violator. In others (for example, medieval Europe), the culture may impose sanctions such as religious excommunication, which are defined as extending beyond the grave.

Whether we realize it or not, we implicitly distinguish norms from one another and define what constitutes violation not so much by the content of the norm as by the reaction of others to its violation. This reaction is not necessarily determined either by the nature of the norm or by the nature of the behavior performed by the violator. The identical behavior may be reacted to by others quite differently when performed by different people or at different times. For example, a sexual relationship between unmarried persons of opposite sexes may be just that, or it may be considered statutory rape, depending on the age of the female partner and regardless of her consent. Trading off sexual favors for material benefits may occur in either prostitution or marriage. When we examine the norms of any society, it behooves us to look carefully at what people do in various circumstances as well as what they say. To use an axion of the enforced sociologist of law, the law is what gets enforced in the courtroom and on the streets and is never quite the same thing as what appears in the law book. This aspect of norms will be more fully explored in Chapter 6.

Internalization of Norms

Any discussion of norms is implicitly a discussion of the phenomenon sociologists call "social control," or the ways in which a society secures conformity to its norms. Social control is largely a product of the fact that men live in social communities and groups in which they are dependent upon one another for their very survival as well as for a variety of material and emotional rewards. For example, a child depends on his parents for food, clothing, shelter, affection, and teaching; each of these dependencies permits the parents to exercise a degree of control over the child. Some social controls (such as those prescribed by law and enforced by police) are overt, but the vast majority are those which come into being as a result of social organization, or the ways in which men live together.

The most effective of all the social controls on our behavior are those which society teaches us to impose upon ourselves. Inhibitions or requirements which we *want to* conform with are far less likely to be violated than those which are imposed on us by threats of the policeman's club. Most norms are *internalized* (incorporated within ourselves) as we absorb our society's ideas of *propriety*. When we know that a particular behavior we have learned is proper, we want to exhibit it ourselves. Once we do this we have set up within ourselves rules for behavior which will rarely be broken. Most folkways and mores are internalized this way, and, as a consequence, most members of a society conform to its norms. This is one way that social control operates. The internalization of norms is a learning process and hence is intimately related to a phenomenon called "socialization." We may explain this phenomenon by saying that as the individual internalizes the norms of a society he is becoming socialized into its culture. The so-called mature adult in any society is one who has thoroughly internalized its norms. (Socialization will be discussed more fully in Chapter 3.)

Ideal and Statistical Norms

One final set of distinctions must be made about the nature of norms in order to avoid confusion. Earlier we used the word *norm* to mean "rule" (that is, a norm is a rule concerning a people's "design for living," which is their culture). We said that a norm could be explicit (North Americans eat with forks rather than chopsticks) or implicit (it is improper to stand very close to someone when speaking with him, except under exceptional circumstances). But the word *norm* is also used in the English language to refer to anything which is typical or average, as in the teacher's phrase: "The norm for this test is . . . " In this usage *norm* is related to the word *normal* and the idea of *abnormality* is related to uncommonness or infrequency. But the two usages are often confused in both popular and social scientific discussions of human behavior, particularly with reference to abiding by rules. The confusion arises because there actually are two kinds of norms which should be distinguished from one another.

The kinds of norms we have been discussing until now can be called *ideal norms*, because they refer to implicit or explicit cultural ideas about how people ought to behave (whether they actually do behave that way or not). An ideal norm is either prescriptive (telling people how they ought to behave) or proscriptive (telling people how they ought not to behave). In this sense, any norm which states a rule for behavior or a definition for the use of a thing or act can be called an ideal norm. Often the members of a society will be aware of many of these as rules and will be able to state them specifically.

A statement of what really is typical or average may or may not approximate the ideal norms. It may reflect phenomena which differ significantly from what is viewed as ideal behavior. This statement of the way the world works could be called a *statistical norm*, since it describes a kind of numerical average. Thus, a statistical norm is a general statement about average or standard behavior. (For example, a certain incidence of suicide is considered "normal" in a society even though it may be defined as undesirable.)

Confusion occurs between the two kinds of norms for many reasons.

1. The existence of ideal norms usually produces conforming behavior; therefore, statistical norms also are usually in accord with them.

2. Deviation from ideal norms may be defined as "abnormal"

(bad) by a society regardless of whether or not it is common or "normal" in a statistical sense (adultery would be an example of this in the United States).

3. A deviation from custom may become defined as "abnormal" and therefore bad even in the absence of ideal norms prohibiting it (for example, long hair for men).

4. People are not always realistic about their own behavior, so it may be popular to believe that people do behave in the way ideal norms say they ought to behave, when actually they do not behave this way at all. (For example, most people believe they are law-abiding when in fact they probably violate some law—often deliberately—almost daily.)

The confusion between statistical and ideal norms is sufficiently common that it is worth-while making the distinctions between them simply in order to clarify our own thinking about normative behavior. Of course, any serious consideration of normative behavior raises questions about abnormality or deviation from both the ideal and statistical norms. In the same way that *normal* has two meanings for human behavior ("in accord with the rules" and "typical"), so *deviant* or *abnormal* also has two meanings ("departing from the rules" and "atypical"). The two usages are often confused. A more detailed discussion of deviance will appear in Chapter 6.

The Sacred Character of Norms

As suggested by the above discussion, norms are important to people in any society; and the necessity for abiding by them may be seen as significant for the preservation of the society itself. Thus, deviation may be viewed as a threat, and deviant behavior may be reacted to with a ferocity which seems out of proportion to the actual behavior involved. Some controversies of recent years concerning flag "desecration" are cases in point. The reason for this ferocity toward norm violators is that people internalize norms so deeply that society's rules become a part of their very being. Thus, a perceived threat to the ideal norms is experienced as a personal attack. The French sociologist Emile Durkheim says that the norms become sacred, holy, regarded with the awe and reverence that men reserve for the supernatural. Durkheim sees religion essentially as a celebration of the social group, the psychic community of a culture, and in particular its moral order.[9]

The sacred character of norms is probably best seen in those which become ritualized. As Durkheim points out, the function of ritual in social life is to create and sustain the sense of the sacred. Thus, anything considered sacred by a society is likely to become ritualized, while simultaneously anything ritualized is likely to be considered sacred (which explains the significance of the flag as a symbol to Americans). Ritualized norms are the norms which represent what is most dear and most ultimate in value to the members of a society. The way rituals function to contain, represent, and make sacred deeply-held social norms can be illustrated by the ceremonies with which American presidents take office, particularly by the extreme case of the inauguration of Lyndon B. Johnson after President John F. Kennedy was assassinated in Dallas.

The American president is a powerful symbolic figure in the United States, not just because he currently occupies the single most powerful office in the world but because he represents the nation's people in both a physical and a spiritual sense. Since the president is invested with this significance, the turning over of office from one president to another (particularly under the circumstances of an assassination) represents a time of national vulnerability and crisis.[10] This is implicitly recognized in the

---

[9]   Emile Durkheim, *The Elementary Forms of the Religious Life* (Glencoe: The Free Press, 1947).

[10]   This is so because the transfer of power is one of the principal and inescapable political problems of any organized government. It is a problem the Roman Empire never solved, and its failure to find a solution contributed to its chronic instability (which also haunts the Soviet Union, among other modern states). In the United States, this problem has been resolved by the institutionalization of the two-party election system. However, this solution has been called into question by increasing public distrust of the parties as being viable avenues for change.

ceremonials which have come to represent the inaugural of a new administration and which constitute its legitimation to us and to the rest of the world.

The ceremonial elements of inauguration are so important that they were included even in the inauguration of then-Vice President Johnson in the immediate and chaotic aftermath of the tragedy in Dallas. Consider the following.

1. Vice President Johnson was sworn in as President within an hour of the official confirmation of President Kennedy's death, thus assuring the nation of the continuity of leadership in a time which could have been one of great crisis.

2. The actual ceremony, although private, was conducted by a federal judge using the traditional Bible, thus symbolizing the legality and "sacredness" of the act, the sanctity of the oath, and the trust thereby transmitted.

3. Members of the former administration were present at the ceremony, and pictures recording the fact were immediately transmitted to the wire services, which served to show the public and the world that the legitimacy of the new president was accepted by the aides of the former one. (Traditionally an outgoing president rides with the president-elect to the latter's inaugural.)

4. Members of the press also were present at the ceremony; in this way the public was, in a sense, present. (Large numbers of people usually attend an inauguration.)

5. Immediately upon returning to Washington, the new President was met by personnel from the State Department and Supreme Court, which further legitimated the new leadership. Then the new President announced on television that he was calling into conference members of the Congress and the Joint Chiefs of Staff; by this act he contacted the other power bases in the government and further demonstrated the legitimacy of his accession to the presidency by assuming

that he had the right to call on them and that they would respond.

6. Finally, immediately after President Kennedy's funeral, the new President held a formal reception for representatives of foreign powers, an act which legitimated his assumption of office, this time to other nations.

Each of the six moves of the new President has traditional duplicates in our ceremonies of presidential inauguration. Each of the ceremonial rituals attests to the significance of the norms it represents, in this case norms about the presidency and what it means, about the necessity that a claim to office be legitimate and be accepted as such, and about the social order which is threatened during any transfer of power. We may conclude that the significant norms of a society are likely to be ritualized or ceremonialized in some way and that if we examine a society's ceremonials, we will learn about the norms which its members hold sacred because they represent the society and are essential to its well being.

Suggested for Further Reading

Ruth Benedict, *Patterns of Culture*
D. W. Brogan, *The American Character*
W. J. Cash, *The Mind of the South*
Clyde Kluckhohn, *Mirror for Man*
Oscar Lewis, *Five Families*
Warren Miller, *The Cool World*
W. H. Whyte, Jr., *The Organization Man*
Laurence Whylie, *Village in the Vaucluse: An Account of Life in a French Village*

Topics and Questions for Discussion

1. A group of university students are arrested on a charge of trespass. Specifically, that during a protest sit-in, they refused to vacate the student union building which had been ordered cleared of people and closed by the university administration. The arrested students together with a number of other students, faculty members, representatives of the press, and representatives from the local community argue that the arrests were illegal, that the protesters were merely exercising their Constitutional rights in accord with the traditional values of the academic community. Other students, faculty members, and townspeople are enraged at the protest and call for disciplinary action including expulsion of the arrested students. What is a sociological explanation for such differences in opinion and interpretation of agreed upon facts?

   One of the factors involved in poverty in the United States is unemployment, particularly among slum dwellers, and one of the chief factors in unemployment, among the young, at least, is lack of education. (For, as unskilled jobs have all but disappeared from the labor market, the proportion of jobs requiring relatively high educational levels has increased.) Despite these facts, "dropping out" of high school remains a widespread practice among young slum dwellers, particularly among males from ethnic minorities. The lack of education thus engendered determines that they will remain slum dwellers and in poverty.

2. It often seems to middle class Americans that such behavior on the part of the poor is not only irrational but deliberate, for "anyone who wants work can get it," and "if they chose to leave school that's their problem." The sociologist, however, would suggest that the situation is not so simple. Explain the relationships implied above between socialization and stratification. Why, in other words, does the lower class reproduce itself and fail to adopt middle class values of "obvious" utility?

3. Deviant behavior may be seen as a reasonable response to perfectly normal social situations. Support this view.

4. Peace corps volunteers have sometimes experienced disorientation upon returning to the U.S. after their two years abroad. Recently, reorientation programs (such as tours of college campuses) have been used to give the returnee a chance for readjustment to American life. Use the concept of culture and other related ideas (e.g. norms, culturshock, mores, acculturation, etc.), to explain this phenomenon.

5. It is not uncommon today to hear about the "cultural deprivation" of underprivileged classes in our society or in emerging or "underdeveloped" nations. It can be argued, however, that the concept of cultural deprivation, as used in these senses, is meaningless. Defend this position sociologically.

6. "Facts are meaningless except in a context of interpretation." Explain *why* this statement is true through reference to chapters 1 and 2.

7. There is a tendency in American society to regard persons who deviate from common culture norms as being neurotic, sinful, or even, in extreme cases, treasonous. The public reac-

tion to the protesters or demonstrators at the 1968 Democratic convention is an example.

Utilizing the relevant concepts in Chapter 2 *describe as a sociologist* (1) what the demonstrators did which created the police and public reactions, and, (2) why the public reaced as it generally did in commenting the police and condemning the demonstrators.

Important: you are *not* being asked to make a judgment on the events in Chicago, only to analyze them by putting them into a sociological perspective using the ideas of Chapter 2. Do not attempt to "go beyond" the events in Chicago themselves, e.g., "after years of demonstrations, people are tired of them." Stick to what happened there and make a cultural analysis of it.

8. Culture and social organization pervade every society (in a sense they *are* society) and are almost invariably taken for granted by the members of a society. When deviations occur, therefore, they are apt to be defined by many people as being bizarre, pathological, and perhaps dangerous. More than one sociologist has noted, however, that social deviation is a normal or natural activity, "an integral part of all healthy societies."

As a sociologist, (1) how can you account for (explain) the viewpoint held by "many people?" (2) explain why sociologists may hold a different view.

9. It has often been suggested that the large university (or "multiversity") has contributed to a certain sense of estrangement (or anomie) on the part of the individual student. Develop sociological arguments to (1) explain why this might occur (perhaps particularly during the first year in residence), and (2) explain what the university might do to alleviate the situation.

Chapter 3

Socialization and Personality Development

The Self Is a Social Product

In the preceding chapter we considered the significance of the concept of culture for understanding human behavior; we concentrated on what can be called the objective aspect of culture, treating it as an external phenomenon. In this chapter we turn to the subjective aspect of culture, which is the human personality and its social nature. If personality is the subjective aspect of culture, then culture is an objective aspect of personality, for cultures cannot exist without people to perpetuate them. The self (the personality) is a social and cultural product.

This concept is sometimes difficult for Americans to comprehend because we grow up in an individualistically oriented society that teaches us to define ourselves as independent entities possessing an essence called "identity" which marks us as unique and special. This definition is accurate in one sense; but in any ultimate analysis it is obvious that we are created by the society and culture in which we mature, so that what we are is a product of our interactions with others in the context of our culture. Indeed, we find upon examination that great portions of what we consider our unique identity really consist of our relations with others. Further, "identity" and its uniqueness, of which we are all so proud, are learned. This chapter will describe how that learning takes place and will attempt to indicate why self is the product of social interaction instead of something unique for each of us.

Language and Socialization

The process through which human infants become social beings and members of their societies is called socialization. A useful synonym for this process is "acculturation of the individual," since what happens is that the culture is impressed upon a young human who initially has none. In the course of this socialization process the personality is acquired (or learned); thus, social scientists regard socialization as a vitally important phenomenon. The vehicle through which socialization takes place is language. Using language (and its learning and use) as his frame-

work of analysis, George Herbert Mead, a philosopher-sociolo-
gist of the early part of this century, described a three-stage
process of development through which the human personality
passes in the course of its maturation. Mead called them the
stage of developing self-consciousness, the play stage, and the
game stage.[1] After describing the initial socialization of the
child, we will elaborate on these three particular stages of personality development.

The Symbolic Nature of Language

There are perhaps only three fundamental ways in which people
communicate with one another: through *pointing*, *signs*, and
symbols. Pointing occurs when one person directs the attention
of another to something through an act which brings the second
person's sense perceptions into contact with that which is being
perceived (for example, by touching it). Pointing, then, consists
of initiating the perception of one person through some outside
intervention by a second person. Pointing is not a form of language and may not require words.

A sign is learned; it consists of an individual's recognition of
the association of two or more events in nature. For example,
dark clouds are a sign of rain. Man does not invent the relationship; it is "out there" in the world.

Like signs, symbols are also learned; but symbols differ from
signs in that the relationship between the elements composing
them is invented and arbitrary instead of existing in nature. For
example, to Christian cultures the cross is a religious symbol

---

[1]   Other leading students of human personality development besides Mead have
perceived three principal stages through which the normal personality is seen to pass.
Freud related the stages to psycho-sexual development and called them oral, anal,
and genital. Piaget, a Swiss psychologist, studied children at play and described three
increasingly sophisticated levels of rules for game-playing. The particular content of
the models is probably less important than the fact that these men saw the process in
terms of three important developmental stages and described the typical "mentality"
at each stage similarly. See Sigmund Freud, *An Outline of Psychoanalysis* (New
York: W. W. Norton & Company, Inc., 1949); Jean Piaget, *The Moral Judgment of
the Child* (London: Kegan Paul, Trench, Trubner & Co., 1932); and George Herbert
Mead, *Mind, Self, and Society* (Chicago: University of Chicago Press, 1934).

that evokes certain meanings, implications, and values. To other cultures the cross may be a simple geometric form without any religious connotations. Thus, the association between the cross and the meaning it has for Christians is invented and must be learned before it can have any importance. The association between events related by a symbol *is* its meaning, and that meaning is invented by man and transmitted through learning. A symbol becomes significant to us when we have learned its meaning. Before that learning takes place, we might recognize a given phenomenon as being symbolic, but it would have no other significance for us. There are, then, two crucially important features about symbols. They are invented (that is, the relation between the symbol and the thing, event, or idea symbolized is an invented one), and their meaning is in that invented relation. In other words, a symbol is meaningful to the degree that we are able to invest meaning in it as a consequence of learning.

Since symbols are related arbitrarily to the things they symbolize, we are taught the meaning of the relation by others in our culture; this social process can be instantaneous and simple or drawn-out and complex. The example of musical notation may be particularly instructive. Whether we read music or not, most of us would recognize that sheet music is paper covered with oddly shaped symbols which have long been used to denote musical sounds and operations. However, if a particular sheet of music had no title on it, someone who did not read music would be unable to distinguish a Brahms etude from some popular tune of the 1940s. That is, he would recognize the symbol system as that of musical notation; but he would have no idea of its meaning, and the symbols would have no significance for him. On the other hand, if the same sheet of music were examined by an orchestra conductor, he would probably be able to recognize not only what piece of music was denoted but also how it would sound if played by his orchestra; the symbols would be so meaningful to him that he would be able to hear the music in his head.

Meaning, then, is social in that it is invested by men in an arbitrary relation between a symbol and an idea or thing and in that the significance of that relation is then transmitted to others. Whoever stumbled upon the idea of musical notation had to invent meanings for his symbols and then teach those meanings to others in order for them to be able to understand the symbols in the way intended by their inventor. Meaning is an agreement or understanding between the creator of a symbol and those to whom it is directed as to what the symbol stands for—the things, ideas, or events which it symbolizes. In the absence of such understanding, a given symbol is recognized as being a symbol, but it has no significance for the person to whom it is directed.

The agreement on what a symbol stands for comes about through learning common usages for it, through being taught to respond in the same way to symbols which are alike. In this sense, meaning consists of a shared tendency to respond to a given symbol in a given way. In a pragmatic sense, the meaning of either a sign or a symbol is the response it gets. People react strongly against flag-burners even though a flag is "just a piece of cloth." This is so because the burning of a flag has symbolic value based on the symbolism of the particular piece of cloth.

Consider the following example of shared response to a symbol. Let us think of a member of the class of objects denoted by the common English word *chair*. Most people have never actually experienced the same chairs as the author has (that is, have never seen, touched, or sat in the identical chairs). In thinking of the word *chair* the author immediately pictured the typing chair in which he sat while writing this book; others undoubtedly conjured up visions of a wide variety of chairs. Yet there is one sense in which everyone's experiences of chairs overlap. This could be called the "lowest common denominator" of the word's definition. My dictionary defines *chair* as "a seat, usually moveable, for one person. It usually has four legs and a back and may have arms." In a sense, this meaning is contained in all chairs and all uses of the word, since we have all experienced that minimal understanding of what a chair is. To that extent, our life histories have overlapped and we have shared the same experiences. This is true also of many other words in the English language. Using a common set of symbols (such as a particular language) involves people in shared experiences. The actual use of a symbol in a given speech, for example, initiates the same general response in both the speaker and the listener. I respond to the word *chair* with my experience concerning chairs; and to the degree that we share identical meanings for the word, through our common understanding of language, my writing of this word stimulates identical reactions in others. Thus, meaning is the shared tendency to respond.

Meaning is social in another sense. The use of symbols for a shared system involves initiator and receiver in the tendency to respond similarly to these symbols, since communication depends on the initiator taking the role of the receiver. For example, if I wish to evoke a particular response from another person, I must select, out of the very large number of symbols available to me, the ones which I think will produce the desired response; then I must use these symbols in a certain order for them to have that result. I can do this only by asking myself, in effect, "If I were he and wanted me to do something, what would he have to say to get me to do it?" Having selected the symbols which would elicit the desired reaction from myself if directed at me, I can then direct them at someone else, with the reasonable expectation that he will react in the predicted way, because we speak the same language (that is, we give similar *meanings* to the same words). If I ask a stranger at a lunch counter to pass me the mustard, he will not hand me the sugar; he has learned the same meanings that I have, since he speaks the same language. Anytime we use symbols, then, we are involved in or responding to a number of different social transactions. Indeed, the use of symbols at all is a peculiarly human and social endeavor.

Symbols make humanness possible, because man is, above all, a symbol-using animal; no other life forms use symbols. From the instant of birth we are surrounded by and submerged in a symbolic environment. In many ways, this environment is far more important to us than the physical environment in which we live, because symbols give us the meanings of things. For example, symbols enable man to live in time in a way in which no other animal ever can. For other animals, every instant is the same, and only one time ever exists, the now; that is, other animals are conscious only of the immediate present. Through language, however, man can put himself into time and know past and future (to some degree); he can adjust his present behavior in the light of the past and in order to bring about a desired future. This would not be possible without the use of the symbols we call words. Try for a moment to think about the future without using words in that tense or the words *tomorrow* or *next*. Difficult, is it not? It can be done. One can, for example, say "the day after today" or "the day which follows this present one" to stand for tomorrow, but it is awkward and takes some doing; and it would be impossible to think about the future without any words at all. Many things of everyday interest today could not even have been thought about by men a few years ago for lack of words to symbolize them. Symbols are the tools of thought, and thought is what differentiates man from other animals (which is not to deny the reality of animal mental processes).

Language and the Development of Self

We saw earlier that taking the role of another is implicit in the use of symbols. Every time I address any symbol to someone else, no matter how rudimentary the symbol is, I implicitly put myself in that person's place before directing it. In doing this, I find out how the other person will respond so that I may select the proper symbol to use in order to elicit the reaction I seek. The use of symbols, then, is a social process, an interaction with others. In the process of interacting with others through the use of language symbols, we develop our personality.

Of course, an infant does not learn his language all at once. Indeed, the constant talk directed at him almost from birth is at first not understood as symbolic. If he perceives the verbal noises about him at all, they must appear at first as signs. They are attached, in his perception of things, to certain events or objects or people in exactly the same way as dark clouds are attached to rain. Later, he begins to acquire the meaning of words and, just as important, the norms and values which his society attaches to the events for which they stand. The following is a description of this process of socialization.

An infant is helpless and entirely dependent upon his mother (or someone standing in that social relation to him) for the satisfaction of all needs and for all the care he receives. He bathes when she wants him to, eats when she gives him food, and goes to bed (if not necessarily to sleep) when she puts him there. Most mothers treat their children in ways deemed appropriate by their society, in accordance with its norms. To some extent this treatment is self-conscious, an attempt on the part of the mother to secure rewards from others for "how nicely baby is dressed" or something of the kind; generally, however, it is entirely unconscious. The mother behaves in accord with her understanding of propriety, because it is "the right thing to do" (that is, because she has internalized the norms herself). This behavior of the mother enforces the same norms on the infant, who is helpless to resist. As a magnifying glass gathers together the diffuse rays of the sun and focuses them upon a spot predetermined by its lens curvature, so the mother gathers together in one spot the norms of her society and focuses them upon the child as a result of her obligation to care for him and "bring him up properly." Throughout every interaction she has with him from morning until night, she talks to him, surrounding him with words and directing a stream of explanatory, descriptive, and emotionally supportive symbols at him. These symbols are the child's most important learning devices concerning the world around him.

Consider the baby-talk symbol *no-no*, probably the word most frequently heard in our culture by toddlers between the ages of seven and twelve months. To the baby, no-no means he is prohibited from doing either what he is now doing or what he is about to do, and he learns the word first as a sign. No-no, is *in* many of the acts in which he engages—throwing oatmeal on the floor, pulling the cat's tail or reaching for the shiny object his mother uses to iron clothes. Every time he does any of these things, his mother says no-no and removes him from the scene of his activity. The baby does not understand why this happens; nor does he understand the arbitrary and invented character of the word *no-no* itself. For him, prohibition is attached to each of the acts in question in the same way that dark clouds are attached to rain. That is, the baby learns the word and its association with his actions, even though he does not understand the character of those actions.

In learning the word this way, the baby acquires something else besides the meaning of the word. He learns from his mother's tone of voice each time she says no-no what her emotional state about the activity is. This emotional state is a personalized and subjective maternal version of the value the social system places upon an activity. The no-no that greets him when he throws his cereal bowl on the floor for the fourth time in one day is likely to be said with entirely different inflection from the no-no which responds to his pulling the cat's tail. In the first case the word probably indicates frustration, impatience, and perhaps an implicit prayer for the strength to refrain from murder. In the second case it probably indicates the mother's sympathy for the poor cat and a desire for baby to "be kind to animals." Thus, as words are addressed to him, the baby begins to acquire both their meanings and the norms and values of his society.

As the child matures, he begins to talk himself; in so doing, he acquires for himself the same meanings and values that his mother has been unconsciously teaching him. The child learns who he is by using the same language to describe himself that others have used in talking to him (since at first they are the only words he possesses to depict himself). In using language this way, he takes the role of the other toward himself and sees himself as an object or event in the world as well as a subject. He calls himself "you" or addresses himself by name, because that is what others have always done (no one ever calls anyone else "I" or "me"). While knowing perfectly well that "you" or "Dickey" is himself, he also learns that he is "you" as used by others—an object as well as a subject. He becomes conscious of himself.

The Stage of Developing Self-Consciousness

The stage of developing self-consciousness, the first of Mead's three stages of personality development, is apparent in most children by the age of two. It is the product of language use and learning and the social and psychological interactions which necessarily accompany them. As an example of a child's behavior at this stage, consider the following. The child approaches the television or hi-fi and reaches out a hand to twirl the dial (as he has done many times in the past). Suddenly, he slaps himself on the wrist with his other hand and says, "No-no, bad boy, mustn't touch!" It is clear that the act of reaching for the dial has stimulated in him the same response which his action had previously elicited from someone else. In reacting to himself as he has learned others will react to him, the child has internalized the role of someone else; he has made the other a part of himself and has become conscious of himself in the same way that others are conscious of him. In other words, he has become self-conscious, an action which is possible only through the use of language. Language is the medium which allows us to see ourselves as others see us and to consider ourselves as objects as well as subjects.[2]

The metaphor of the theater is commonly used to make this point. The self can be viewed as consisting of two parts, subject and object (or actor and role). The subjective aspect of self is the actor, the "I" which initiates, plans, and experiences. The objective aspect of self is the part played by the actor, the "me" which others observe acting out the initiatives of the actor. The "me" consists of a number of roles (for example, student, son or daughter, sister or brother, Catholic or Methodist) while the "I" thinks about these roles and acts them out.

---

[2] It is exactly this point which marks the fundamental difference between human mentality and that of other animals. Animals are conscious. But, unlike men, who possess a language, the animal does not know that *he* is conscious; he is aware but does not know that it is *he* that is aware. An animal may be hurt or hungry, but he cannot be aware that it is *he* who is hurt or hungry.

The Play Stage of Personality Development

The child begins to play at about the same time he begins to develop self-consciousness. The play stage, as Mead refers to it, is the second major growth stage of the human personality. The types of play engaged in and the mentality which makes them possible continue to illuminate the function of language and society in forming the human personality. *Play* is a word which covers a number of different activities at different ages of life. Mead uses the word to distinguish the free recreation and entertainment activities of the younger child from games, which are organized by rules. (The child cannot learn to play games until he has gone through the play stage of development.)

Each year of age is apt to see profound differences in the kind of "play" a child can perform. A toddler of perhaps eighteen months may play by taking pots from the cupboard, nesting them one inside the other on the floor, and then putting them back into the cupboard again; six months later this fascinating pastime will have lost all its charm. The play of very young children is likely to be simple, mechanically repetitive, and solitary. Toddlers do not play with one another cooperatively. They may play in each other's company, but the activities will usually be uncoordinated (except in the sense that one may build a pile of blocks which the other will then knock down in order to enjoy the ensuing uproar).

As the child grows up, his verbal ability increases and his play takes on increasingly organized form. At the age of three, a little girl having a tea party with her dolls and teddy bear may vary her voice range from high squeaks to low growls in order to play all the roles her task requires. She may also move to stand behind each "actor" as she plays his part. A year later she will probably conduct the entire enterprise from one spot and in one voice. At the age of three, she needs the physical differentiation in order to remain clear in her own mind what role she is playing at any instant; by the age of four, she can maintain the differentiation mentally without difficulty. She has reached a level of verbal organization where she can manipulate the various roles without physical action.

The significance of play, once it becomes organized by any

sophistication of verbal ability, is that it is likely to involve the child in a great deal of role-playing. Children from four to eight years of age spend large proportions of their free time in play, often in imaginative role-playing of one kind or another. Cowboys and Indians, mothers and fathers, fairy princesses, soldiers, firemen, and teachers are all common roles assumed by children in play. Psychologically speaking, the child learns two things through this kind of activity. He learns to play the adult roles he sees around him, and he learns who he is by "being" who he is not. He tries out the different roles, seeing how it might be to have one role or another or to feel or act out a particular emotion. In this sense, play is probably a significant preparation for later life.[3]

All the roles in children's play are those of particular others —a fireman, a mother, a fairy princess, and so on. Models for these roles come from television, storybooks, and daily life. They are always concrete, in the sense that the child is imaginatively imitating some person, character, or occupational role as seen from his own viewpoint. His role-playing is fluid, subject only to the limitations of his own understanding of the role. While he may play in the company of others cooperatively, they do not determine the character of the role played. That is, a child can define his own role as a cowboy, for example, without reference to the way another child acts out his role as an Indian. He adjusts his behavior to the other child's in order to keep the play going, but the *character* of the roles played is independent. The play requires only transitory agreements between the children as to the general outlines of their behavior.

The Game Stage of Personality Development

When the child reaches about eight years of age, a new level of personality development appears. This level, which Mead called the game stage, is the third and final stage of personality devel-

---

[3] Play also acts as an emotional release for children, enabling them to "work out" feelings they could not express in the situations originally eliciting them. I am reminded of the time I scolded my three-year-old daughter and chased her away from the cookie jar. She began to play with her teddy bear, telling him to help himself to imaginary cookies in an empty coffee can and urging him to take all he wanted.

opment. It is manifested by the child's ability to move from the unorganized free-form activity of play to the mental and verbal organization demanded by and incorporated in games.

In play, roles are free, fluid, and independent of each other; games, however, are organized by and constituted of rules. That is, in play a child can do and be what he wishes, and other players can adjust their behavior accordingly. For example, if two children are playing cowboys and one decides to switch from being a good guy to being a bad guy, it need not interrupt the play at all. When it becomes apparent what he has done, the other child can change his behavior too, and the play can go on. But in games, the roles are related to each other by rules which define what those roles are and how they are to be played; the rules also define the object of the game, the limits placed upon the players, the "ground" upon which the game is to be played, and so on. In free play, the action is the play; in a very profound sense, however, games *are* rules. In play, the meaning of the role is what one does with it. In games, however, the meaning of the role is defined by the rules of the game. In perhaps the most simple and universal of all games, hide-and-seek, there are only two roles—hider and seeker—although more than one person can take either role and any number can play the game. But there is no meaning in hiding if no one seeks or in seeking if no one hides. *Thus, in games the meaning of one role lies solely in its relation with the other roles; it has no meaning outside that relation.*[4]

The reason game-playing symbolizes a new stage of personality development is that the player, in order to do his part, must know the roles of all the other players and adjust his behavior generally to theirs (while in the play stage he needed to know only one role and could vary it as he chose). The game of football illustrates the need to know others' roles in order to play the game properly.

[4] As shown by that feeling you got in the pit of your stomach when you were young and the big kids agreed to let you play hide-and-seek with them if you would be "it"; and you counted to one hundred and then looked and looked, endlessly it seemed, until finally it dawned on you that while you were counting, they had run away.

When a quarterback is deciding upon a play to call, he must take into consideration not only what might work but also how every man on the field has been performing, the ground position, score, time, down, weather, and so on. In making his decision (deciding his role), he must adjust his behavior to these factors within the limits permitted by the rules. He cannot solve a pass defense problem by shooting the defender he wants eliminated. In order to make his decision, the player must adopt the role not of *particular others* but of a *general other*; he must assess his expectations all other players and of those possibilities dictated by the roles. The player must know the roles of all other players simultaneously, as a response to the total situation in which he finds himself. The significance of games to the social development of the human personality lies in its duplication of the individual's experiences in the social community. Most people organize their behavior with reference to their expectations of a generalized other, which is, in fact, their understanding of how the society expects them to behave.

Students often show a general uniformity of dress in the classroom. When one group of students were asked if they selected their clothing in response to the known expectations of some particular other person (for example, to please a boy friend or girlfriend), most answered no. What, then, accounts for the uniformity? Clearly, the students dressed according to a general expectation or understanding of what is appropriate, of what unspecified other people expect; this is an indication that the customs of the society, the community, or the general other had become integrated into their personalities.[5]

To put it another way, society becomes a part of us because of our learned understanding of its expectations, which we internalize in our personality structure. We learn this understanding through language, and we integrate it into our person-

---

[5] When mother asks, "What will the neighbors think if you wear these grubby clothes?" she rarely is referring to the people next door or across the street. After all, these people should know you and therefore not be impressed by your clothes; and if they do not know you, they should not care anyway. If challenged, mother would probably reply that she didn't really mean the neighbors but rather other people in general (the anonymous "they" to whom people refer so much of their behavior).

ality through the use of language. Thus, language makes us social through an involved learning process in which we internalize the values and expectations that constitute the normative system of our society.

Reference Groups

As described earlier, the society or the social community to which we belong becomes part of us through language and through our internalization of its norms. We absorb these norms from what Mead called the generalized other. Groups also are a part of us, in a more self-conscious way; we call such groups "reference groups"—that is, groups of people who we use as an example of how to gauge our own behavior. Essentially, two kinds of reference groups exist. There are groups to which we already belong, whose norms we desire or feel constrained to meet, and there are groups with which we identify emotionally or psychologically whether or not we become members of them. (For example, recording groups may be imitated in clothing, mannerisms, and so on even by those who have no expectation of adopting that occupation.)

In either case, the individual has some perception of norms which he identifies with a reference group; he judges his behavior against this standard and modifies it as necessary to achieve the behavior he perceives as ideal. The norms of the reference group are internalized because the individual finds that attaining (or maintaining) the perceived standards is emotionally desirable or necessary. In this way, even groups to which one does not belong may deeply influence his behavior. Reference group behavior as a source of emotional satisfaction sometimes functions in bizarre ways (as when extermination camp inmates imitated the manners and clothing of their Nazi tormenters).[6]

In summary, the individual and the society cannot be considered as separate entities. The American concept of individual-

---

[6] See Elie A. Cohen, *Human Behavior in the Concentration Camp* (New York: W. W. Norton & Company, Inc., 1953) and Primo Levi, *Survival in Auschwitz* (New York: Crowell-Collier Publishing Company, 1961).

ism often separates the two, considering them to be in conflict with each other (a popular theme in literature and drama is that of the individual versus the group, state, or society). But in a sociological sense, no final distinction can be drawn between the two. Societies must have members in order to exist, and individuals cannot exist without societies. The society is contained within the individual; that is, the society's norms exist only in our understanding and are revealed only by our behavior. This internalization of norms produces the collective behavior which constitutes society. We reproduce the norms in others through the use of language, thereby perpetuating both society and "humanity" (that which makes us human).

Society and individuals, then, are two sides to the same coin, and both must exist in order for the coin to exist. A coin with one face blank is not a coin but a disk of metal; a society without members or individuals without socialization cannot exist. Although they can be analyzed separately, the two are indistinguishable in nature.

Suggested for Further Reading

Erving Goffman, *Encounters*
Erving Goffman, *The Presentation of Self in Everyday Life*
W. E. Grier and P. M. Cobbs, *Black Rage*
John Howard Griffin, *Black Like Me*
Abraham H. Maslow, *Toward a Psychology of Being*
David Riesman, *Individualism Reconsidered*
Samuel A. Stouffer, et al, *The American Soldier*
Anselm Strauss, *The Social Psychology of George Herbert Mead*

Topics and Questions for Discussion

1. Because of biological differences, men and women play different roles in society. Defend or oppose this viewpoint. Use evidence from the text to support your answer.

2. From the point of view of society, socialization is the way in which the individual is fitted into an organized way of life. This statement assumes the group as forming the basis of social life, and sees the shaping and adapting of individuals *to* groups as a significant social phenomenon. But *self* is created through socialization and interaction with others. Thus our social groups, particularly primary groups, *become part of ourselves*.

   Explain the implication of these facts upon the popular notion that "anyone can make it in the U.S. (i.e., achieve success, become upwardly mobile) if he tries hard enough."

3. George Herbert Mead argues that there are neither human minds nor selves without society. Develop an argument or essay supporting this contention utilizing the concepts of Chapters 2 and 3.

4. It has often been suggested that the large university (or "multiversity") has contributed to a certain sense of estrangement or anomie on the part of the individual student.

Develop sociological arguments to (1) explain why this might occur (perhaps particularly during the first year in residence), and (2) explain what the university might do to alleviate the situation.

5. Socialization seems to be responsible for a person's concept or understanding of himself. If a person considers himself a deviant or a criminal is, it the socialization process that is responsible for this view or is it the person himself?

Chapter 4

The Organization of Society: One View

In the last chapter, we said that personality is the subjective aspect of culture and that the group becomes part of the personality through internalization of norms. In another way, we can say that groups are among the objective aspects of culture. While culture itself is an abstraction, the behaviors of social groups and the results of group membership are objective. It is important to integrate some of the concepts already presented and to relate them with others in order to understand the structure of society.

We explained earlier that sociology is one of the generalizing social sciences and that it obtains its data through the process of empirical observation. We suggested that sociology usually generalizes about some aspect of culture but that culture can never be observed directly. We described how culture becomes a part of individual behavior (which can be observed directly) while at the same time producing it. We conclude from this information that the raw material of sociology is the observation of human behavior and its effects, whether we are interested in individuals or groups. As with culture, a group also is an abstraction. For example, there is no way of observing "familiness," since a family consists of certain relationships among people and not just a group of people of certain ages and sexes. In observing group behavior, we see the behavior of individuals who are relating to one another in certain ways.

The sociologist is not interested in all human behavior; he is concerned only with social behavior. Specifically, he observes what can be called *social actions*. A social action is any human behavior which is oriented either directly or indirectly to other people. The act of eating is not a social action; but what is eaten and when, how often, with what implements, and with whom one eats are all social actions. Social actions comprise the behavior which the sociologist observes when studying the world, and he generalizes from such observations. The other matters of

---

* "One View" has been included in the chapter title in order to draw attention to the fact that other sociologists might quarrel with some of the description or terminology. Sociology is a way of looking at things, and different sociologists often see them differently.

sociological interest are all abstractions developed from collections of observed social actions or inferences made from them.

The distinction between what actually is observed and what may be inferred from the observation is the basis of what was once called "dust bowl empiricism" (which limited itself to what could be strictly observed). The following anecdote is an example of this empiricism. Two sociologists were riding a train. On looking out the window, one of them observed that the sheep in a field they were passing had been sheared. "Well," replied the other, "all we know is that they have been sheared on the side facing the train." This appears to be absurd; however, the sociologist must remain aware of the distinction between what actually is observable in social behavior and what may be reasonably inferred. In the sense of this anecdote, the sociologist is always looking at the world out of the window of a train. He cannot explore minds to determine why people really behave as they do. He can only ask them why and then either accept their word, interpret it to suit the facts as he sees them, or make inferences on the basis of what he sees. So the basic realities of sociology—the "lowest common denominators"—are simply the observable actions of individuals, which are oriented to others. On the basis of dozens or hundreds or thousands of observations of such social actions, the sociologist sometimes infers that they are part of more complicated social events. Thus, a group can be viewed as a collection of individuals displaying social actions which are so frequent and have such similar consequences that, taken together, they constitute a unit. When we look at the unit, we infer the existence of a group, but we *see* only a collection of individuals displaying certain repeated patterns of social action.

The Interrelation of Social Actions, Norms, Roles, Groups, and Institutions

We said earlier that the smallest unit of sociological understanding is the social action. Since social actions are the only observable phenomena, all larger or more inclusive behavioral concepts must be composed of or reducible to them. However, sociologists constantly speak of observing groups. Indeed, groups are so common a social phenomenon that it makes sense, as a kind of shorthand usage, to talk about them as if they were actual entities rather than inferences made on the basis of observation.

A group can be defined as three or more people interacting together over time in an orderly way on the basis of similar expectations for each other's behavior.[1] This regularity over time provides the pattern of social actions common to the group. The expectations for behavior shared by the group members provide the regularity for observed social actions, which in turn are the product of shared norms. The norms are learned through socialization into the same culture or into the particular roles of the group. Roles are particular collections of expectations for behavior based on position in the group. For example, family members all share some expectations, because they have all learned similar role expectations for people in particular positions in the family group (that is, mother, father, and so on). Thus, the regularity of social action which constitutes the pattern of a group is the result of its members sharing similar expectations for each other's behavior, based on socialization in cultural norms and roles.

Groups can be perceived as collections of roles, and roles can be perceived as collections of expectations. The sharing of expectations for each other's behavior makes social actions predictable, and this predictability makes it possible for the group to exist. For example, the family could not exist as a group if there were a reasonable expectation that at any time one member might attempt to murder another. People can interact with one another regularly only if they are able to predict each

---

[1]   It takes three people to make a group because that is the smallest number in which one member may be substituted for another without destroying the collective entity. In a dyad (a two-person collectivity) the substitution of another person for one member produces a new and different dyad; with three or more people the substitution of one member need not change the interactions between members in any essential way. Two-person interactions carried on over time become so personal that such substitution is impossible without changing the entire nature of the relationship.

other's behavior with some degree of success. One of the major accomplishments of the socialization process is the indoctrination of each member of a culture into the roles which will be expected of him in adult life and into the relationships between his and other's roles. When a person encounters a situation not covered by his early socialization (for example, induction into an army or rushing by a fraternity), his role relationships are immediately taught to him by members of the group involved. Military basic training or fraternity pledging are in good part training in role relationships.

Why do people fulfill role expectations? What motivates them to learn and perform roles? The answer is that roles—individual aspects of group membership—are of great significance to everyone. Roles are a vital part of our identity; in addition, they enable us to survive by securing the necessary cooperation of others in providing us with food, clothing, shelter, and so on. To illustrate this point, try the following simple exercise.

Take a piece of paper and, in one minute, write down as many answers as you can to the question "Who are you?"

Now examine the answers you gave to that question. Notice that most of the answers you gave consist of the roles you play—student, son, Baptist, male, and so on. Indeed, it is rare for people to answer such a question with anything except a role.[2] This suggests the importance of roles to us. Who we are is one of the most private and subjective questions we can ever be asked, and overwhelmingly we answer it in terms of the roles we play, that is, in terms of our group memberships in society. Our identities are defined in terms of the groups to which we belong.

---

[2]   This is an exercise I have often used in the classroom. Normally, about 95 percent of the answers given there are roles or statuses (statuses will be explained later in this chapter), and most of the remaining 5 percent turn out to be errors. For example, it is not uncommon for someone to answer, "alive," but this is an incorrect answer to the question of who one is. An example of a correct answer which is not a role would be "I am a human being."

Group memberships are important for another reason. If we know what roles a person plays, we have learned a great deal about him and can predict his behavior with considerable accuracy. For example, if we are told that a person is an American, a Catholic, a white, a husband, a son, a schoolteacher, a father, a city-dweller, a Republican, a member of the VFW, an alumnus of Yale, and a member of Rotary, we have learned and can guess a great deal about him. We can predict with reasonable accuracy his income, level of housing, consumption patterns, taste in reading matter, level of family health and medical care, political attitudes, sexual values, and even projected life span. We could guess probable causes of his eventual death and the likelihood of his divorcing his wife. Thus, group memberships have tremendous significance for the individual and for his interactions with others. In a real sense, they *are* self; the roles we take from them are who we are.

Social Institutions

In every society, similar groups (such as families or military units) tend to behave in similar ways; for example, each society recognizes certain ways of relating to one's mate or of waging war. These broad patterns for social behavior are called social institutions. A social institution is not a group. The institution of the family is not a particular family; in any society, the social institution of the family is a description of the ways in which families are expected to behave, the standard arrangements of roles within them, and their standard relations to other groups and institutions. For example, the family institution in the United States has traditionally been patrilineal (family relationship traced through the male, virilocal (place of residence determined by the husband), and to some degree patriarchal (father dominant in decision-making). These characteristics, along with others, provide the pattern of interaction typically followed by people playing the family roles of husband, wife, and child. This pattern of normative behavior is the institution of the family; it is acted out by real people living together in actual groups called families.

Institutions themselves are deeply interrelated. For example, the family has a great deal to do with economics and to that extent is a part of the economic institution. (Only within this century in the United States has the family ceased to be the basic productive unit of our economy, and it remains the basic unit in much of the rest of the world.) Since all the principal social institutions of a society are interconnected, the family also has important ties to military, religious, charitable, and educational institutions in most societies. These interconnections between social institutions constitute the social structure of a society and give it a "strain toward consistency," as one sociologist has phrased it.[3] (That is, there are parallel patterns in the interlocked institutions.)

Social Structure and Social Organization

We have said that the social structure of a society is based on the interrelationships of institutions. In any society, the central institutions must be interconnected in such ways that they work as parts of one another. The phrase *military-industrial complex*, for example, points to the interrelations in the United States between military and economic institutions. It is inevitable that social institutions will be interconnected, but the ways in which those connections are made vary immensely. Consider what kinds of interrelations might be called to attention if we were to examine the military-industrial complex of the Plains Indians in the year 1850. Warfare among these Indians was supported economically by the individual fighting man, who supplied his own weapons, horse, and food, while depending on the country through which he moved to supply forage for the horse. In the same period, the United States cavalry was supported economically by the government, which purchased supplies for the soldiers from individuals and corporations with money collected from people and organizations by taxation. We can see from this example that the social structures of the two

---

[3]   William Graham Sumner, *Folkways* (New York: Dover Publications, Inc., 1906).

societies were quite different with regard to the support of warfare.[4]

If we perceive social structure as the operation of institutions in relation to one another, then we can perceive social organization as the expression of social structure in the individual's life (that is, the ways in which people act reflect institutional interrelations). For example, my position as the head of an American family imposes on me the duty of providing economic support for that group, since that is part of the social structure of our society. In order to fulfill this obligation, I have a job and earn a paycheck which I use to provide for my family. The adjustment of my life to this requirement is part of the social organization of my life because it is a near-universal requirement of the society in which I live.

Social organization, then, is the individual's life pattern that grows out of his interactions with others and that is dictated by his group memberships, and groups are visible embodiments of social institutions. Another way of looking at the matter is that social organization consists of the adjustments and arrangements we make in order to do what the norms embodied in our social institutions require us to do. Social organization is social structure acted out.

Status

Status is a special kind of role acquired from membership in social categories which are considered significant by one's culture, rather than from membership in particular groups. Statuses are universal roles, some aspect of which every member of a culture enacts. For Americans the most important statuses are age, sex, and race; marital status and some occupational statuses are only slightly less significant. Each of us has a sex status, an

---

[4]   It is an interesting footnote to history that although both societies used a form of cavalry, the Indians' tactics were of superior quality, and the army quickly adopted them with modifications for more organized use. In fact, the fighting techniques of the Plains Indians are reflected today in the armored (tank) doctrine of every army in the world.

age status, a marital status, and a race status. Statuses are *what* we are, the socially significant categories by which other people identify us and by which we identify ourselves.

Roles reflect group memberships; statuses reflect identity characteristics. A person may *belong to* a family, a church, or a football team, but he *is* young or old, married or single, and white, black, yellow, or brown. Roles are relatively specific; their performance is based on the expectations of others, and each person is evaluated on the adequacy of his performance. Statuses are generalized; they are considered to be social characteristics rather than performances, and each person is evaluated on the basis of his attitudes toward possessing them. A role can be dropped or changed. A status cannot be changed or abandoned; it is attributed to an individual by others, and he cannot affect it.

Conventionally, there are two kinds of statuses, ascribed and achieved. A status is a cultural category by which all of us are defined. As such, status is ascribed. There are some statuses which we can choose whether or not to adopt; however, once we make the choice, we cannot change it, since these statuses then have become a part of our identity in society. For example, I can choose to become a husband; this reflects my membership in the social relationship of marriage. I am also free to reject this relationship through divorce, that is, by dissolving the condition which it reflects. I can also choose to become a father, but once I have done so, I can never undo it. I will be a father for the rest of my life. Fatherhood and motherhood are achieved statuses, although the husband-wife relationships which create them are roles, and all of these are or may be related to one's marital status, which is ascribed. Each of us is either single, married, widowed, or divorced. Certainly occupations also partake of achieved status as well as group membership in the form of roles. Physicians, priests and professional soldiers, for example, are all treated in ways which suggest that their occupational choice has given them a social identity which, say, the insurance salesman does not have. Similarly, great fame may impose an achieved status upon someone who previously had played a simple occupational role (as when a politician becomes president or an actor becomes a superstar). Statuses are *what* we are; roles are *who* we are.

Statuses are more important to us than all of our roles together, because they determine how our society will define us and, therefore, what is likely to happen to us. They have great influence on what Max Weber called "life chances," the probability of different possible occurrences in our lives (dying at an early age, going hungry, obtaining a particular kind of job, and so on). Statuses determine life chances because they are tied to groups. Race status is important in American society because it expresses the institution of caste; marital status is important because it reflects the institution of family. Statuses can be perceived as institutions in action, in the same way that roles can be perceived as groups in action. Statuses are broad, categorical, general, and impersonal. They are not specifically connected to groups, although the institutions to which they are related reflect and determine the relations within and between the groups in a society. Many norms express themselves in terms of statuses (for example, norms relating to ladylike behavior).

One of the effects of the link between norms and statuses is that many of our everyday interactions with others are performed on the basis of status (that is, we relate to others as male or female, old or young, and so on). This may be depersonalizing, but it is also inevitable to some degree. It is quite possible that the only way we can get through a day is by treating many of the people we encounter as statuses (or even functions). Consider the complications that would pervade our lives if we had to relate and react to everyone with whom we interacted (for example, the man who pumps gas into the car and the girl who sells newspapers in the lobby) as if they were relatives or friends. It would be impossible to get anything done, since we would have to spend considerable time interacting on a personal level with everyone we encountered. Instead, a significant proportion of our daily interactions with others are status interactions. Indeed, we find it disturbing when something occurs that alters such exchanges, as when a personal remark is made during an interaction supposed to remain impersonal.

Status and Ranking

Up to this point we have considered status as expectations for behavior in a way similar to our conception of role. Now we will also consider status as ranking on the social ladder. All statuses are ranked in a society (although not necessarily with reference to one another); in fact, the word *status* commonly implies ranking as well as role. Status as ranking involves two dimensions—social deference or prestige and the relative value placed on categories within a status. The social deference aspect of status is used to describe people as being of high or low status. An example of the relative value component in the United States is that it is generally considered better to be male than female, young than old, white than nonwhite, and so on. Most discussions of status as ranking involve more of what we have called role in descriptions of high and low status rankings than our usage here would permit. Certainly achieved status and some roles to which ranking are ascribed are familiar to us. "Criminal" and "aristocrat" are examples of these two usages.

Rank itself, as in a military rank, is an achieved status (although it typically has strong role components), and it always reflects the stratification hierarchy of some organized group. In other words, it refers to a hierarchy level within that group. In sociological usage, one has rank as a consequence of certain kinds of group membership, although the group in question could be a feudal aristocracy, in which case rank and status in the society (than status as ranking sense) might be nearly parallel. A rank is not a position in a group, but in some groups, positions are ranked.[5]

---

[5]   It is unusual to find groups which use rank but do not rank all the positions within them. When this does occur, as with the use of civilians by the military in military contexts, it is often necessary to give the interlopers assumed or quasi-ranks in order to locate them in the system. Further, since the purpose of such ranking is the creation of an unambiguous order of superiority and subordination, formal systems of rank usually are worked out so that no two members of the group can have exactly the same rank. In the United States Army, for example, among officers of the same military rank, the one who was first promoted to that rank is senior; of men of the same rank and date of promotion, the one commissioned longest is senior; and

Suggested for Further Reading

Thurman Arnold, *The Folklore of Capitalism*
John K. Galbraith, *The Affluent Society*
Michael Harrington, *The Other America*
Robert S. Lynd and Helen M. Lynd, *Middletown in Transition*
Robert Nisbet, *Community and Power*
David Riesman et al, *The Lonely Crowd*
George Simmel, *Conflict (and) The Web of Group Affiliation*

Topics and Questions for Discussion

1. Socialization is the process by which one acquires culture and forms his self-identity. Yet aspects of social stratification in society may or may not support the identity formed through primary group socialization. How does stratification affect one's self-perception? One's identity?

2. Socialization is the way in which culture is transmitted, and the individual is fitted into an organized way of life. Socialization inevitably produces a degree of conformity. Discuss some of the factors which encourage individuality and uniqueness.

3. Identify and briefly describe the social organization of your own life utilizing the sociological data and methods which have been presented in the first four chapters.

---

among men of the same rank, date of promotion, and length of commissioned service, the oldest is senior. An interesting variation on this usage is academic "rank," which is really a status designation for it is neither a position nor a rank in a military sense. Academic rank is somewhat related to pay, but it has no functional significance in a hierarchial way. Senior professors cannot order around junior professors by virtue of their rank; some junior men are paid more than some senior men; and all professors perform more or less identical functions regardless of rank. (See Chapter 2 of the author's *Academic Janus* (San Francisco: Jossey-Bass, Inc., 1971.)

Chapter 5

Social Stratification

In the last chapter we suggested that people can be ranked relative to one another on the basis of their statuses in society. The phenomenon of ranking is known technically as *social stratification*. All human societies, even the simplest, have levels (strata) of social rank as one of the mechanisms influencing how their members relate to one another.[1]

Stratification traditionally is based on four variables—status, class, caste, and rank (in the sense of organizational or feudal hierarchy.) We will not deal here with the last of these, as it is simply a variety of status which we have already discussed. We have seen how status can act as a stratification variable, how people can be ranked relative to one another according to the honor or deference they receive in a society. Thus, status is one standard dimension of social stratification. Although people are ranked on the basis of their statuses, the statuses normally are not ranked relative to one another. In the United States it is considered better to be white than nonwhite, better to be young than old, and better to be male than female; but it is difficult to say whether it is better to be an elderly white female or a young nonwhite male. We may agree that generally it is better to be a physician than a worker, but who has higher status—a female physician or a professional football player? Thus, we can see that people are ranked on the combined value of their statuses, but the statuses themselves are not ranked. The remainder of this chapter will concentrate on stratification in social class and caste.

Social Class

Social class is a term used to classify people according to the rewards and privileges they possess as a consequence of their

---

[1] This observation may provoke controversy among social scientists. However, I am aware of no human society (historic or contemporary) in which social ranking of some kind does not occur; and ranking *is* stratification. There probably are classless societies, but *social class* is a special term with a well-defined meaning that includes, but is not limited to, the notion of ranking. This term will be discussed more fully later in the chapter.

economic standing in society. Class is always involved with
economic factors. It is the way people rank one another on the
basis of financial people rank one another on the basis of financial considerations, the result of social ranking measured by
wealth.[2] Life chances (the probability of any given occurrence
in life) in any industrialized society are also deeply involved
with social class.

For Western special scientists, the theory of social class has
been influenced beyond measures by the work of Karl Marx.
Marx was probably the first important "class theorist"; his ideas
were so fruitful and his observations so insightful that their
impact still colors almost all consideration of class. In a sense,
Marx invented the social scientific conception of class. This is
not to say that all class theories today are Marxian, as that word
is usually used, or that Marx's observations on class, made in the
middle of the last century, still hold true in the world today. In
the United States, his observations on class do not hold true,
and they never did; even in less industrialized and more feudal
areas of the world, they have not gone without correction or
modification. But some of his views remain useful today, particularly his observations that life chances are strongly influenced,
if not determined, by economics and that people seem to fit
into social strata which are economic in character and which
can be characterized by their "relation to the means of production."

Marx suggested that economic forces determine social reality,
that the individual's position in the social system is determined
by economic forces and is the result of his relationship with the
means of production in the society. Marx believed that fundamentally there were only two kinds of economic relationships

---

[2]   Which is why in very simple societies class may not appear as a form of stratification. For example, in some preliterate hunting-gathering societies, wealth in the
sense in which we use the term is unknown, since everyone shares equally in the
technological possibilities of the system. In such societies, foodstuffs are the only
material rewards possible, and they are relatively perishable and always shared in case
of need anyway. The traditional polar eskimos are instructive in this regard. They had
no concept of private property; that is, they did not conceive of themselves as
owning material property at all, although certain nonmaterial items such as songs,
magic, and mana (supernatural power) could "belong to" individuals.

in Western industrialized societies and that the dialectical process of history was moving all societies toward the same industrial model.[3] The two possible relations were those of producers and of parasites. They were represented in the social classes by workers (who produced wealth through labor) and capitalists (who were parasites because they did not create value through labor but instead gathered the wealth created by the labor of others, through their ownership of land, machinery, and so on). Marx saw these two great social classes becoming more self-conscious and aware of the differences in their economic and social interests. He theorized that eventually all workers would realize their exploitation by capitalists, at which time they would join together in a revolution to destroy the economic system which exploited them and would then institute a more benign one—the communistic workers' state, "the dictatorship of the proletariat."

Marxian theory is more sophisticated than this cursory review would indicate, but there were many things it did not take into account. For example, Marx could not foresee the development of either the common stock company on the modern corporate model or of the twentieth century American labor union, which is so different from its European predecessors. However, Marx's importance for the study of social stratification is based on

---

[3] The "dialectic" studied by Marx is a model for social change in the world, the "process of history" developed by the German philosopher Hegel. According to Hegel, dialectical change is the movement from a "thesis" (a statement of fact) to an "antithesis" (a contradiction of the first statement); the contradiction is resolved through "synthesis" (a logical process which removes the inconsistency by reconciling the two positions on a higher level of truth). There, the synthesis becomes a thesis in its turn, generates its own antithesis, gets resolved in a new synthesis, and so on. Hegel saw history as following these "dialectical laws"; but he was also a philosophical idealist who believed that reality as we perceive it is simply an idea in the mind of God. Marx boasted that he "turned Hegel on his head" by denying the significance of ideas as reality and espousing the reality of material phenomena (in this case, economics); thus, he is known as a materialistic philosopher. Marx remained wedded to the idea of dialectical change, however, and in his class theories the capitalist and worker classes are thesis and antithesis which will be resolved in the synthesis of the worker's communist state. At this point the dialectical process of history will end. [The state will "wither away," and historical change will end in Utopia. It is a charming, and romantic, reverie.]

three of his fundamental observations which remain valid today and thus influence current work in this area. These fundamental observations are the following.

1. All societies are stratified.
2. A major basis of stratification is economic; that is, most social strata reflect economic factors, and it is rare for any society's system of stratification to ignore them entirely.
3. In most instances, "relation to the means of production" serves to fit individuals into the economic component of stratification; that is, wealth tends to be related to position in the productive system. Actual possession of the means of production or service, or ownership of the society's natural resources, usually is sufficient to place one at the top of the stratification ladder.[4]

On the basis of these observations it is possible to define four social classes in industrialized societies. These are categories of people who have similar access to wealth, as a result of their relation to the productive system, and who share similar life styles and life chances because of their class position. The four classes are comprised of owners of the means of production or resources, managers of production or resources, possessors of socially useful or necessary skills, and workers (sellers of labor). The following is a description of these classes.

Owners of the means of production or resources. Through ownership, these people control either the natural resources

---

[4] Ownership of tools is sometimes the working man's equivalent of this possession within the working class. It is alleged that Walter Chrysler was able to found the machine shop which eventually became the great auto corporation by virtue of the fact that he had inherited either his tools or the price of them from his father and was thereby able to put "investment capital" into a "plant." One of the chief arguments for unionization in the early part of this century was that the great growth of industry caused workers to lose the freedom to change jobs. That is, workers could no longer own their tools (for example, turret lathes) because they were too large and expensive; thus, they had lost the independence that is a basic assumption of classical economics. Workers in the building trades and auto mechanics in small shops may be the last people to whom actual ownership of their tools still connotes economic independence.

of the society, the tools which are necessary to transform the resources into products, or the services which the society requires in order to function (for example, railroad or steamship lines). As a consequence of their ownership and control of basic necessities, people in this class are able to extract from society the greatest share of rewards available. They occupy top positions in the stratification structure.

Managers of production or resources.   These people are able to extract the second largest share of society's rewards because of their technical value to the owners. Plant managers, finance manipulators, and others run whatever enterprises owners do not control themselves. In the United States they are a powerful class because of the decentralization of ownership and the separation of ownership from control that has been made possible by the stock-held corporation. For example, the owners of such companies as General Motors number in the thousands, but these stockholders do not control the firm or actually run it. Because of their technical expertise at management and control, managers in the modern economy are beginning to supersede owners as members of the top strata, even though traditional Marxian formulations would put them in the number two position.

Possessors of socially useful or necessary skills.   This class consists of professionals, semiprofessionals, clerical people, skilled workmen, entertainers, and so on. Included among them are soldiers, priests, entertainers, athletes, physicians, decorators, teachers, jewelers, and craftsmen. They exist below corporate managers on the scale of social reward they extract from society, but they are above the large group called "workers." They differ from both the managers above them and the workers below them in that they have special skills which are sold to all members of the society; they provide the white-collar and artisan service skills used by everyone. Many of these people are independently employed, and the services they provide are sufficiently universal that horizontal mobility (movement from job to job or place to place within a social class) is not difficult for them. In modern societies their occupations are also apt to provide avenues for upward social mobility (movement up through the stratification levels). Their level of reward is based on the value society places on their services, and little direct control is exercised over their activities by those above them in the stratification system. Persons with government or industrial bureaucratic skills are coming to be important representatives of the class in all modern societies.

Workers—sellers of labor. At the bottom of the stratification system of all class societies are those people whose only resources for procuring rewards is the sale of their energy (manpower) or crude skills. These are the unskilled and semiskilled workers or laborers. In most nonindustrialized societies, this group has comprised the largest single class; indeed, in most societies it is larger than all the others combined. However, this is no longer true for the United States, and it is increasingly less true for other developed nations, as the "tertiary" or service occupations increase in economic significance. Historically, life chances among the workers have been meager and their quality of life low. According to Thomas Hobbes, an English philosopher, their life has been "nasty, brutish, and short." The industrial and managerial revolutions have changed these conditions considerably in all of the industrially developed nations of the world; however, in much of Asia and Latin America, and in parts of Africa, Hobbes's description is still apt. In the United States, jobs for laborers have disappeared very rapidly during this century. (While they represent perhaps 90 percent of the typical work forces of the rest of the world, unskilled or semiskilled laborers now constitute less than 15 percent of the American occupational force.) This decrease in unskilled and semiskilled jobs has inflicted great hardship on the remaining laborers who have been dispossessed (particularly the nonwhites) and has created pockets of appalling poverty amidst sparkling plenty. But the disappearance of these jobs is not peculiar to North America; it is a product of industrialization and the managerial revolution of production all over the world.

These four categories of people can be seen as a model for the traditional social scientific conception of social class (or socioeconomic class, as it is sometimes called to emphasize the economic basis of the distinction and to diminish the significance attached to "breeding" or "society"). Of course, the categories are not exhaustive; some people and positions do not fit any of the categories, and some exceptions to the general description exist. Yet, most societies can be more or less described in these terms; an observer of their structures could classify the populations on the basis of these four groupings without greatly distorting social reality. In general, the four categories represent economic classifications which are determined by or are functions of Marx's "relation to the means of production," and it is unusual for the relations between and among them to be upset. (For example, most workers actually do receive a lesser share of economic rewards than most managers, although occasional exceptions can be found.) The United States does not fit the model as well as the older European economies do, since those remain closer to the economies from which the original Marxian model was drawn. Also, the soviet Union in some respects resembles the United States more closely than it does czarist Russia in its economic organization, despite the "communist" nature of its system.

For our purposes, the importance of this model of social classes is not that it is accurate in every particular but that it suggests the relationship of class to the individual's life chances.

Social Class and Life Chances—An Example

We said earlier that social class is important because it strongly influences so many of the individual's life chances. An illustration of how class affects a particular kind of life chance—public school experience and its effects upon the child—will graphically demonstrate its importance.

In the United States, the significance of education for occupational placement, upward social mobility, and so on, can hardly be exaggerated. Education has been one of the traditional routes for upward social mobility, the mechanism which makes it possible for an individual to free himself from some of the social limitations of his birth. To the extent that the United States has an open class system, the public school probably has been largely responsible for the fact that it remains open. The atio Alger myth unquestionably exaggerates the possibility of "lifting oneself by one's bootstraps," particularly if one is nonwhite. However, upward mobility has been and remains possible, particularly when it is tied to educational competence and certification. Education, then, is a life chance which significantly affects most of us. If the school experience is influenced by class (and there are a number of strong indications that it is), then that relationship is of immense importance.

Sociologists are becoming even more aware of the significance of the subculture of class among the student body for educational outcomes and aspirations of students attending particular high schools. All schools have student subcultures of various kinds—athletic, academic, delinquent, and so on.[5] But many urban schools also have subcultures of class based on the predominant social class of the students who attend them. The effect of these subcultures on the educational and occupational aspirations of the students is profound. Lower class students who attend predominantly middle class high schools are much more likely to aspire to college training and professional occupations than are their peers in predominantly lower class schools. Similarly, middle class students who attend predominantly lower class schools are less likely to value college or aspire to professional careers than are *their* peers elsewhere. Social class thus influences life chances by coloring the high school experience in such a way as to affect what one learns to want or to expect from life.[6]

Class also influences educational outcomes by its effects on the attitudes of teachers and administrators toward students of different class backgrounds. It frames the educational expec-

---

[5] See James S. Coleman, *The Adolescent Society* (New York: The Free Press of Glencoe, 1961).

[6] In this respect, what one is taught to expect may be more important than what one wants. For example, if a student wants to become a doctor but believes that he can never do so, he will be extremely unwilling to try. One of the key problems of inner city education is that of motivating lower class students of all ages to aspire to expectations they have learned to ignore. Remember that culture is, in many respects, in one's head.

tations of both teachers and students, and it directs the sch.
curricula to the predominant class of students. A recent
discovery about the American public school is that it shows a
rather strong bias in favor of the middle and upper class
students and against those of the lower class. The schools have
not been deliberately designed that way (as some have charged);
the bias exists because the vast majority of the people who
control the schools are middle or upper class themselves. W.
Lloyd Warner, an anthropologist, summarizes the results of a
number of studies of the class origins of high school students
and instructional personnel, as follows.[7]

Class Origins

	Lower Class	Middle or Upper Class
School board members	6%	94%
School teachers	6%	94%
Pupils	60%	40%

With the above distribution of class origins for school board
members and teachers, it is easy to see why the schools are
biased toward middle class values and definitions of reality and
why they are to some extent "alien lands" for lower class students. The middle class bias operates in a variety of ways.
Schools in upper and middle class neighborhoods are likely to
be newer and better equipped; they tend to have better librar-
ies, science laboratories, and classroom equipment than schools
in lower class areas. Upper and middle class parents, who share
the educational values of school administrators, take more interest in the schools than lower class parents. They are also more
likely to make their voices heard on matters of school policy,
materials, and curriculum. (Hyperactive PTAs do not exist in

---

[7] W. Lloyd Warner, _American Life: Dream and Reality_ (Chicago: University of
Chicago Press, 1963), Chap. 8.

anti thesis

slum neighborhoods.)[8] Similarly, upper and middle class parents can and do exert pressure on their children's teachers. These teachers are in an extremely vulnerable position, because in most school systems there are no effective tenure systems and the teacher's job may become a political football at any time he or she becomes "controversial." So if a parent makes it plain that his child is to receive more attention, special coaching after school, or something of the kind, the child is likely to receive it either voluntarily from the teacher or at the "suggestion" of the principal. In either case, the school structure twangs like a bowstring in response to parental pressure. Such pressures are much less likely to come from lower class parents, who usually are either indifferent to the school and the child's progress in it or else passively accept anything done to him there. Further, even if the lower class parents are interested in the school, they typically have no influence which might be brought to bear against it. Whose child will the teacher spend extra time and effort on, the doctor's or the truck driver's?

Perhaps best known of the ways in which the public schools have built-in class biases is the matter of curricular materials. Books, teaching machines, models and illustrations, records, and so on have been and remain today largely slanted toward the upper and middle class student. Judging from my own students, about two-thirds of contemporary college students had "Dick and Jane" as their first reader. Who were the principal characters of that series? They were white middle class children who were always clean and scrubbed; they lived in a "nice" neighborhood with large lawns and play equipment, and they were often taken on expeditions to shops, museums, and places of industry. To what extent does the world represented in this

social bias

---

[8]   The PTA represents an interesting quasi-official school auxiliary, often mobilized by shrewd administrators to favor their own policies, so that it becomes an extension of the administration's (principal's or board president's) influence. But because the PTA is the vehicle of organized parental interest in the school, it may also be mobilized as a pressure group *against* the school by interested or disgruntled parents. In either case it serves as a communication channel through which parental opinions and pressures may be exerted. It is quite successful in middle and upper class neighborhoods and notoriously failure-ridden in lower class neighborhoods.

series reflect the reality of the typical American child, much less the child from the lower class urban slum or from another country? The typical first reader in the American school is now racially integrated (that is, one of the kids has had his face painted brown), but it still does not reflect at all the realities of life on city streets, in urban slums, in ethnic ghettos, or in Appalachia. In other words, many curricular materials still are not designed for the majority of the children who have to use them. (What use is a globe to a child who has no conception of either models or maps?) Historically, curricular materials have tended to ignore students who were not white middle class and often even those who *were* white middle class but of recent immigrant origin. Only a few years ago the state of Texas discovered that Mexican-American children were really no more stupid than Anglos. It was found that they simply spoke a different language; and when they were instructed in that language in the schools, they competed very well with English-speaking students. The lesson still has not been learned with perfect clarity in Texas, much less in New Mexico, Arizona, and California, where these children may still be thought to be stupid.

Another familiar bias in the schools is the "track system," in which overwhelmingly greater prestige has always been accorded to the college preparatory curriculum. This "track" has the lion's share of the budget and the best teachers, materials, and classrooms. The students in the college preparatory track usually are of middle and upper class origins, while the vocational and commercial tracks are filled with students from the lower class (even though assignment to the tracks is supposed to be made without bias).[9]

Finally, teachers tend to favor upper and middle class chil-

---

[9]   See *The Autobiography of Malcolm X* (New York: Grove Press, Inc., 1964). Malcolm tells how, even though he was a good student, when he told a teacher he wished to be a lawyer, he was "counseled" to attempt something more realistic, such as carpentry. And this author can still recall his own amazement at the student composition of a "dumbbell" English class to which he was once assigned. The students defined it as a "dump for the dumb, deaf, and delinquent" and were not much off in the categorization; similarly, the teacher was also a reject.

dren, whose backgrounds are similar to their own. The typical middle class white female teacher finds that her upper and middle class students, who share her values, offer far fewer discipline problems than do the lower class children. Based on her experience and training, the teacher has a certain conception of what behavior is appropriate to the classroom, and she tends to favor the children who manifest it and to regard as ill-behaved those who do not. The consequence of this conception of appropriate behavior is that the lower class child gets caught in a vicious circle, where his normal behavior, values, and demeanor are defined as inappropriate, and he is punished for them. The more he is punished the more hostile and resentful he becomes, and he is likely to behave aggressively, resist discipline, and so on.

The teacher, on her part, is largely unprepared by her own upbringing and professional training for this kind of child. She can only call upon her knowledge of what "ought to work," which is, of course, derived from middle class values and behavior patterns. She isolates, scorns, and scolds the recalcitrant student. The more she disapproves of him, the more aggressive he becomes; this aggression is met with greater and greater discipline and restraint. The child becomes more negative toward school as it is made increasingly unpleasant for him. His reputation as a troublemaker develops and gets passed on from teacher to teacher, so that as he progresses through the grades each one is "ready for him" when he appears. He becomes a truant and eventually a dropout, and he is supported in this by his culture and his peers, who define school as a waste of time.

The human tragedy of the situation is that for the child who confronts this educational experience, school has indeed been a waste of time. The social tragedy is that the middle class biases of the school have pushed the child back into his neighborhood culture almost as forcefully as his cultural values have pulled him away from the school. And the outcome, of course, is that by dropping out of school the child closes the door on almost any opportunity to change the conditions of his life. Upward mobility is largely denied anyone in American society who does not have at least a high school diploma. Thus, the neighborhood school, acting through its administrative and educational personnel, reduces the possibilities for individual upward mobility. As a result, the class structure remains less "open" than it might otherwise be. The operation of these limitations on mobility is coming to be widely recognized, and some colleges and producers of educational materials are beginning to take steps to remedy the situation. A great deal remains to be done, however, to change the class bias of the public school and to alter its effect upon the maintenance of the class structure and its implications for life chances.[10]

Class and Behavior

For the sociologist, social class is important because it is intimately related to a variety of other behaviors, including the life chances an individual encounters. Social class is related to, and in some cases determines, language, religion, entertainment, occupation, sexual patterns, consumption patterns, and even definitions and understandings of reality itself. Consider the simple matter of eating. What one eats, where, and how all vary greatly from home to home in the society, but certain similarities exist within each social class. For example, the proportion of income spent on food, the proportion of that food budget spent on meat and dairy products, and the proportion of diet devoted to cereals are sure guides to social class. That is, the lower classes are likely to eat a larger proportion of cereals and a smaller proportion of meat and dairy products than do the upper classes.[11]

The intimate relationship of even insignificant details of liv-

---

[10] Readings which graphically illustrate the life of slum dwellers are Oscar Lewis, *La Vida* (New York: Random House, Inc., 1965); Piri Thomas, *Down These Mean Streets* (New York: New American Library of World Literature, Inc., 1967); and Claude Brown, *Manchild in the Promised Land* (New York: The Macmillan Company, 1965). All contain pointed references to the failure of the public school system in regard to the slum child.

[11] See Jean Fourastie, *The Causes of Wealth*, trans. Theodore Caplow (Glencoe: The Free Press, 1960).

ing to social class membership is so well known and so stable and easy to document that one sociologist developed a method for measuring class membership which was based on simple observation of a family's living room. Reproduced here is the 1931 Chapin Living Room Scale with score values for different items of construction, furnishing, and so on. A second scale (not reproduced here) gave similar scorings for the condition of the room and its contents (articles strewn about in disorder, −2; in place or in usable order, +2).[12] When properly followed by an observer, this simple check list gave consistent and reliable measurements of a family's social class position. Whether the living room was also used as a bedroom, whether the sewing machine was in it, and whether the pictures on the wall came from calendars were very important—if mundane—clues to social class membership.

Scale for Rating Living Room Equipment

I.   Fixed Features

1   Floor . . . .
    Softwood 1, hardwood 2, composition 3, stone 4.

2   Floor covering . . . .
    Composition 1, carpet 2, small rugs 3, large rug 4, oriental rug 5.

3   Wall covering . . . .
    Paper 1, kalsomine 2, plain paint 3, decorative paint 4, wooden panels 5.

4   Woodwork . . . .
    Painted 1, varnished 2, stained 3, oiled 4.

5   Door protection . . . .
    Screen 1, storm door 1.

6   Windows . . . .
    1 each window.

7   Window protection*
    Screen, blind, netting, storm sash, awning, shutter, 1 each.

---

[12]   F. Stuart Chapin, *Contemporary American Institutions* (Dubuque: William C. Brown Company, Publishers, 1948), Chap. 19.

8   Window covering* . . . .
      Shades 1, curtains 2,
      drapes 3.

9   Fireplace . . . .
      Imitation 1, gas 2,
      wood 4, coal 4.

10   Fire utensils . . . .
      Andirons, screen,
      poker, tongs, shovel,
      brush, hood, basket,
      rack, 1 each.

11   Heat . . . .
      Stove 1, hot air 2,
      steam 3, hot water
      4.

12   Artificial light . . . .
      Kerosene 1, gas 2,
      electric 3.

13   Artificial ventilators 1

14   Clothes closets 1

Total Section I . . . .

II.   Standard Furniture

15   Table . . . .
      Sewing 1, writing 1,
      card 1, library, end,
      tea, 2 each.

16   Chair . . . .
      Straight, rocker,
      arm chair, high
      chair, 1 each.

17   Stool or bench . . . .
      High stool, foot-
      stool, piano stool,
      piano bench, 1 each.

18   Couch . . . .
      Cot 1, sanitary
      couch 2, chaise
      lounge 3, daybed 4,
      davenport 5, bed-
      davenport 6.

19   Desk . . . .
      Business 1, per-
      sonal-social 2.

20   Book cases 1 . . . .

21   Wardrobe or movable
      cabinet 1 . . . .

22   Sewing cabinet 1 . . . .

23   Sewing machine . . . .
      Hand power 1, foot
      power 2, electric 3.

24   Rack or stand 1 . . . .

25   Screen 1 . . . .

26   Chests 1 . . . .

27   Music cabinet 1 . . . .

Total Section II . . . .

III. *Furnishings and Cultural sources*

28   Covers . . . .
       Furniture, table,
       chair, couch, piano,
       1 each.

29   Pillows . . . .
       Couch, floor, 1 each.

30   Lamps . . . .
       Floor, bridge, table,
       1 each.

31   Candle holders 1 . . . .

32   Clock . . . .
       Mantel, grandfather,
       wall, alarm, 1 each.

33   Mirror 1 . . . .

34   Pottery, brass or metal
       Factory made 1,
       hand made 2.

35   Baskets . . . .
       Factory or hand
       made, waste, sew-
       ing, sandwich, dec-
       orative, 1 each.

36   Statues 1 . . . .

37   Vases 1, flowers or
       plants 2 . . . .

38   Photographs 1
       (portraits of per-
       sonal interest) . . . .

39   Pictures . . . .
       Note if original or
       reproduction. If
       original, oil, water
       color, etching, wood
       block, lithograph,
       crayon drawing,
       pencil drawing, pen
       and ink, brush draw-
       ing, photograph
       (when treated as a
       work of art), 2 each;
       if reproduction,
       photograph, half
       tone, color print,
       chromo, 1 each.

40   Books† . . . .
       Poetry, fiction, his-
       tory, drama, biog-
       raphy, essays, liter-
       ature, religion, art,
       science (physical,
       psychological, so-
       cial), atlas, diction-
       ary, encyclopedia,
       .20 for each volume.

41   Newspapers** . . . .
       General, labor, local
       community, sec-
       tarian, 1 for each
       type of paper.

42 **Periodicals** ** . . . .
News (current
events), profession-
al, religious, literary,
science, art, chil-
dren's, 1 each; fra-
ternal, fashion, or
popular story, .50
each.

43 **Telephone** ** . . . .
Switchboard con-
nection 1, two-party
line 2, one-party
line 3. (Note social
or business mainly.)

44 **Radio** ** . . . .
Crystal 1, one-tube
2, three-tube 4,
five-tube and up 5.

45 **Musical instruments** **
Piano 5, organ 1,
violin 1, other hand
instruments, 1 each.

46 **Mechanical musical
instruments** **
Music box 1, phono-
graph 2, player-
organ 3, player-
piano 4.

47 **Sheet music** ** . . . .
Opera, folk, mili-
tary, ballads, classic,
dance (other than
jazz), children's ex-
ercises, .05 for each
sheet; jazz, .01 for
each sheet.

48 **Phonograph records** **
Type of music (as
above); type of in-
strument repro-
duced; voice—solo,
duet, quartet, chor-
us; instrumental—
solo instrument
(piano, violin, etc.),
trio, quartet, band,
orchestra, .10 for
each record; jazz .01
for each.

Total Section III . . . .

---

*If checked out of season, ascertain if used in season and so record.

  †To be recorded if in another room (except professional library of doctor, lawyer, clergyman).

  **To be recorded if in another room.

Source: F. Stuart Chapin, *Contemporary American Institutions* (Dubuque: William C. Brown Company, Publishers, 1948), pp. 383-86.

Many of the items on this scale no doubt seem quaintly archaic, but the scale could easily be updated. The first item, for example, could devote more space to the *kind* of carpet, since carpeting has ceased to be a floor covering found only in expensive homes. The importance of this scale is that it shows how everyday matters are reliable and stable indicators of class membership. Other everyday indicators of social class are magazines read (from which, for example, the predominant clientele of a barbershop can be predicted) and beverages consumed (the upper classes tend not to drink boilermakers). An interesting exercise would be to study grocery stores in upper and lower class shopping districts, measuring the amount of shelf space in each store devoted to such things as cereals and dried beans or the meat counter space devoted to steaks and lamb.

Much more important than any of these behavioral relations to class standing are some of the vital life chances. For example, birth and death rates vary by class, as do infant and maternal mortality rates, life expectation, educational attainment, and vitality (health and illness, including how often certain diseases are communicated and how often they are lethal). *There is practically no life chance which is not in some way related to and influenced by class standing.*

Class affects almost every aspect of our behavior; it is perhaps the most pervasive of all sociological variables, having even more influence than sex on much human behavior. The sociologist is fascinated by the study of class because of this great influence on behavior; in fact, any study of human behavior cannot ignore the phenomenon of class. In a society of absolute universal social equality, social classes would not exist. But thus far no perfect distribution system for material goods has been developed, and therefore we have no "classless" societies (except for certain preliterate peoples still existing at a Stone Age level). Thus, the differential distribution of material rewards *is* a class system; and because this differential distribution is closely connected with access to life chances, it is inevitably associated with behavior distinctions as well.

The Function of Social Class

The almost universal existence of social classes has puzzled sociologists for a long time. Because of the influence of class on human behavior, and its stability, various explanations have been offered for its persistence. Probably the best known explanation is offered by Kingsley Davis and Wilbert Moore. They theorize that class is universal in complex human societies because it serves to produce and maintain the division of labor within them, and they believe that the division of labor is necessary for any such society. Since some tasks (such as farming and health care) are essential to the survival of the society, people must be motivated to undertake them. However, some of these essential tasks are more difficult or more dangerous than others, and some require more skill or training than others. The supply of persons willing or able to perform these tasks will be smaller than for tasks which are less demanding. Therefore, in addition to motivating people generally to do what is necessary, the society must select talented people and motivate them to take the jobs requiring their particular abilities; and it must motivate other people to undertake the long or difficult training which other jobs require. This is accomplished by rewarding some tasks more highly than others, thereby making them more attractive and insuring an ample supply of applicants. If one task is more important to the society than another task, it must be rewarded more highly in order to prevent the other from competing with it equally. Such a system of differential distribution of social reward is *social stratification*. Social stratification persists even in democratic societies devoted to ideologies of social equality because of the need to insure that significant social positions will be filled and conscientiously performed.[13]

This is an appealing and reasonable argument, regardless of its accuracy. It does have weak points, however, and they are important. One of them is the difficulty of defining "important" tasks or of associating existing social reward systems (class systems) with any sensible hierarchy of social importance. In order to exist at all, any society must produce and distribute food to its members, but few societies give high class standing

---

[13]   See Kingsley Davis and Wilbert Moore, "Some Principles of Stratification," *American Sociological Review* 10 (1945): 242-49.

to farmers, food wholesalers, or food retailers. It may be argued that although these tasks are necessary, they are not particularly difficult and therefore do not need to be highly rewarded in order to insure their performance. But not all highly rewarded positions are difficult or socially imperative (airline steward-esses), nor are all similar tasks regarded as similarly essential in all societies. Compare, for example, the high status of the physi-cian in the United States with the lower status of his counter-part in the Soviet Union (where doctors have about the same occupational prestige as high school teachers do in the United States).

Davis and Moore also cannot explain the large range between least and most rewarded tasks in a social system. Even accepting their basic assumptions, the only necessary differential between rewards would be whatever was sufficient to get more impor-tant positions filled before less important ones. Certainly the existing differential between corporate directors and share-croppers is wider than it need be for that purpose. Furthermore, high reward does not necessarily demonstrate the importance of a position or the degree of skill needed to perform it. Finally, perhaps the most telling rebuttal to this theory of class is that class position (and the reward that goes with it) tends to be inherited from one generation to the next, while this is certainly not true for either socially necessary skills or importance of positions. Thus, the social inequality which in one generation may be used as an argument for the identification and utiliza-tion of talent, when transmitted through inheritance becomes an inhibition on the discovery and utilization of talent among the lower classes in the next.

There can be no question that a society's class system often performs services for it in regard to the division of labor, but it appears that the system is not always needed for this purpose. That is, while the division of labor is necessary, a class system to carry it out is not. The question of why class persists is rarely asked today; the fact that it appears to be an almost universal phenomenon may be an adequate answer to an essentially meta-physical question. As we learn more of its importance, its ubiq-uity, and its behavioral consequences, the notion that social

in her tenue

in her tenue

class could be done away with (which is implied in the question of persistence) seems simpleminded. Today, the study of stratification has turned away from questions of that kind and toward the measurement of class, its related behavior, and social mobility.[14]

Caste

If *class* is a form of stratification based on wealth, then *caste* can be understood as a form of stratification based primarily on birth. A caste position is inherited and unchangeable, since it is believed to be genetic or racial. That is, caste is an *ascribed status,,* a cultural definition imposed by others on an individual. Many societies have had caste or caste-like stratification systems (for example, aristocracies), but the two most visible systems in recent history are probably the ancient caste system of Hindu India and the more recent color caste system of the United States. In India the caste system reached its greatest development during the nineteenth century. The four major castes were, in order of descending social standing, Brahmans, Kshatriyas, Vaisyas, and Sudras, with a large number of Untouchables (pariahs or outcastes) beneath them. The caste system was created by the Aryan conquerors of India more than four thousand years ago, and the four major castes probably reflect successive waves of Aryan conquest. By the end of the last century the castes had proliferated into thousands of subcastes, and this

---

[14] Social mobility may be defined as movement through social space. There are three types of movement: *vertical*, or movement up or down class levels by an individual during his lifetime; *horizontal*, or movement within a given level, as from job to similar job or place to place; and *intergenerational*, or changes in level which may occur when children's class levels are compared with those of their parents. In the United States, where competition is the mechanism often used to distribute social reward, there is a great deal of *downward* intergenerational mobility as well as the expected upward mobility. According to the 1970 census, only about 10 percent of the people in the lowest occupational positions had parents who also had occupied such positions; in other words, 90 percent of unskilled laborers had fallen to that occupational level. This indicates that in any competitive system there must be more losers than winners.

stratification affected every phase of Indian life. In the United States the caste system was introduced by the importation of black slaves from Africa, who were largely tribal in origin and culture. Like the Indian caste system, the American caste system is beginning to break down under the impact of governmental pressures, active protest from those who suffer from it, and realization of its unfortunate impact upon all members of the society.

Several general principles seem to exist in any caste society, whether the basis of the caste divisions is racial (as in the United States), religious and occupational (as in India), or inherited political (as in a feudal aristocracy). These principles are as follows.

1.   Caste is fixed at birth, with the individual inheriting the caste standing of his parents (usually his father).

2.   The castes are endogamous. That is, legitimate marriages can take place only *within* each caste, although nonmarital sexual unions may occur across caste lines. In such cases a man might seek a concubine from among women of a lower caste; a reverse situation would be strongly tabooed, because in any male-dominated society the children of a higher caste female and lower caste male would inherit the lower caste standing of the father.

3.   Every major social institution of the society partakes of and reflects the caste system.

We can readily observe these principles of caste in the United States. The American caste system consists simply of whites and nonwhites, although, parallel to the Indian model, it is possible to identify "subcastes" within each group.[15] The castes are culturally defined as a consequence of biology (the races), although this is genetic nonsense. But since the society holds that definition, the individual is born into one caste or another and

---

[15]   For example, Mexican Americans, who are generally either white or an ancient mixture of white and Central American Indian, are treated as nonwhite in many ways; and Jews, who are almost all white, occasionally experience similar treatment. Among nonwhites, Orientals clearly have the highest subcaste status and Negroes the lowest, with Amerinds somewhere in between.

cannot leave it except in very rare cases. Endogamy is the cultural rule, and only within the past two decades has the Supreme Court struck down state laws forbidding cross-caste marriages. As a matter of custom, however, caste endogamy is still practiced in almost all American marriages. Cross-caste unions even of a nonmarital kind are frequently subject to severe sanctions (as taboo violations) from members of both castes.

The ways in which the social institutions of a caste society reflect and support the caste system can be seen in the American case, and general statements about them probably apply with equal accuracy to India or feudal Europe. For example, educational curricula or the school themselves may be segregated for members of the different castes, or those of the lowest caste may have education forbidden to them altogether. Occupations tend to become identified with castes; some occupations are considered appropriate for only the higher castes and are forbidden to the lower castes, while others are considered appropriate for only the lowest caste.[16] Marriage remains endogamous, and cross-caste liaisons are tabooed. Residence is usually geographically segregated. Child-rearing patterns and other family related matters are likely to reflect caste distinctions. Even religion is likely to see caste segregation in places and forms of worship. Religion also may rationalize the continuation of the caste system, as in Hinduism (where a major religious duty was absolute obedience to caste rules), in feudal Europe (where the doctrine of the divine right of kings existed), or in the United States (discussed below).

One interesting fact about the American South is the geographical coincidence between the Black Belt and the Bible Belt. That is, roughly the same area that practices the Southern racial system in pristine purity also has the heaviest concentration of ultraconservative, fundamentalist Protestant-

---

[16]   In the United States there is a conception of "nigger work," as well as a long-standing restriction of nonwhite participation in the professions. In fact, professional and higher managerial positions are still largely "lily-white," and more or less segregated education remains the rule.

ism . . . Protestant fundamentalism, while it is obsessed with the idea of sin, has a curiously limited concept of its extent. Revivalistic preachers thundering against the wickedness of the world invariably fasten on a rather limited range of moral offences—fornication, drink, dancing, gambling, swearing. Indeed, so much emphasis is placed on the first of these that, in the *lingua franca* of Protestant moralism, the term "sin" itself is almost cognate with the more specific term "sexual offence." Whatever one may say otherwise about this catalogue of pernicious acts, they all have in common their essentially *private* character. Indeed, when a revivalistic preacher mentions public matters at all, it is usually in terms of the private corruption of those holding public offices. Government officials steal, which is bad. They also fornicate, drink and gamble, which is presumably even worse. Now, the limitation to private wrongdoing in one's concept of Christian ethics has obvious functions in a society whose central social arrangements are dubious, to say the least, when confronted with certain teachings of the New Testament and with the egalitarian creed of the nation that considers itself to have roots in the same. Protestant fundamentalism's private concept of morality thus concentrates attention on those areas of conduct that are irrelevant to the maintenance of the social system, and diverts attention from those areas where ethical inspection would create tensions for the smooth operation of the system. In other words, Protestant fundamentalism is ideologically functional in maintaining the social system of the American South.[17]

Finally, it is obvious that the political institutions of a caste society are intricately involved with the caste system. Indeed, it would not be an exaggeration to say that the political institution and the caste system are coextensive, for if politics is the distribution of power or decision-making, then caste rules for

---

[17]   From Peter L. Berger, *Invitation to Sociology* (New York: Doubleday & Company, Inc., 1963), pp. 113-14.

behavior must follow the power rules exactly. If they did not, the caste rules would immediately be brought into accord with the uses of power by those who hold it.[18] No social system could work any other way. Thus, we commonly find in caste societies that positions of political significance are either forbidden to members of the lower castes or are permitted only as token participation. We also find that stratification of the power structure follows the caste structure exactly; that is, power is directly associated with high caste standing. A caste system can be regarded as a political system based on birth.

Caste systems work primarily because they are based on custom. India's caste system began with the subjection of conquered peoples by their military conquerors but was soon rationalized by the social institutions which the Aryan conquest generated. The primary rationalizing force was probably the Hindu religion, with the result that the main body of sanctions for caste violations became religious ones. Caste practice in the United States is equally customary, but because we are an essentially secular society, we generally define our caste system as social rather than religious. Thus, sanctions against caste violators are likely to be social, and the expiations and rituals of cleansing which violations entail likewise are social. They range from ridicule and mild ostracism to lynching, but in any case the sanction applied is rationalized as a rite necessary to restabilize the balance of the community (the "way of life" which is presumably threatened by the violation). Sanctions are punishments for offenders as well as rituals for healing the fabric of a social community torn by the offense; and since the system is defined as social, the sanctions are applied by the community rather than the gods.

It probably is not necessary to convince American college

---

[18]   In the early 1960s Stokeley Carmichael used the phrase *black power* to refer to the tactic of bloc voting. It is not surprising that this term frightened many people, for to white America the term *black power* means a radical reordering of the social structure whereby a group now composed mostly of have-nots would become haves. Inevitably this constitutes a threat to the American status quo, since it suggests that many things would change and that those who have may ultimately have not.

students that they do, in fact, live in a caste society, although the thought may well be an uncomfortable one. Like any other form of stratification, caste has deep and clear implications for the life chances of all members of the society (for caste rules apply to all with equal force, even though the behavior demands are different for members of the different castes). The following table is abstracted from the U.S. census. It illustrates the degree to which caste touches our lives and affects some of the most fundamental life chances we possess. We accept the fact that caste is related to occupational differentiation, political disenfranchisement, and educational discrimination. But if this form of stratification is so pervasive and so effective as to create actual biogenic differentials among members of the different castes, then it is powerful indeed. Life chances—and death chances—follow caste lines. No other argument for the existence of a cast system in a given society could be so powerful.

Caste, Vitality, and Mortality in the United States

Life Chances	Whites	Nonwhites
Live birth rate (1968)	81.5	114.9
Life expectation at birth (1967)	71.3	64.6
Number of male survivors to age 65 per 100,000 born alive (1967)	65,990	50,180
Maternal deaths per 100,000 live births (1967)	19.5	69.5
Infant deaths per 1,000 live births (1967)	19.7	35.9
Male death rates per 1,000 by year:		
1900	17.0	25.0
1920	12.6	17.7
1940	10.4	13.8
1960	9.5	10.1
1967	9.4	9.4

Source: U.S. Department of Commerce, Bureau of the Census, *Statistical Abstract of the United States* (Washington D.C.: U.S. Government Printing Office, 1970), pp. 48-55.

Suggested for Further Reading

E. Digby Baltzell, *The Protestant Establishment*
David Caplovitz, *The Poor Pay More*
K. B. Clark, *Dark Ghetto—Dilemmas of Social Power*
Eldridge Cleaver, *Soul on Ice*
William M. Dobriner, *Class in Suburbia*
John Dollard, *Caste and Class in a Southern Town*
Ralph Ellison, *The Invisible Man*
C. Wright Mills, *The Power Elite*
C. Wright Mills, *White Collar*
Gunnar Myrdahl, *An American Dilemma*
Vance Packard, *The Status Seekers*
Lee Rainwater, *And the Poor Get Children*
C. E. Silberman, *Crisis in Black and White*

Topics and Questions for Discussion

1. The Protestant Ethic conveys the idea that hard work and individual initiative are all that are required to get ahead in this country (perhaps plus just a little good luck). Why is this conception ill-suited to the needs and experience of non-white Americans?

2. Assume that massive amounts of federal funds are made available for the relief of poverty so that every American family has a guaranteed annual income of $5,000. Will this solve the problems of race relations in the United States? Will it solve any of them? How?

3. India is governed by a caste system which has rules pertaining to marriage, occupations, and descent. In this caste system a person of high caste becomes polluted if he approaches or touches someone in a lower-caste grouping. It also prohibits the lower-caste from entering temples and schools used by the higher-caste. Show how the American caste system, white and non-white, compares to and is similar to the Indian caste system.

4. If "making it" in American life is defined as achieving business, professional, or financial success, perhaps with attendant public acclaim or fame, explain why persons of the lower social classes may be prevented from "making it" by their class backgrounds. What's wrong with the notion that "anyone can make it if he tries hard enough"?

5. Socialization is the process by which one acquires culture and forms his self-identity. Yet aspects of social stratification in society may or may not support the identity formed through primary group socialization. How does stratification affect one's self-perception? One's identity?

6. One common belief in American society is that anyone, with a lot of hard work and a little luck, can "make it" from rags to riches. Using your knowledge of such concepts as social status, stratification and social mobility, is this belief an ideal or a social reality? In other words, is social stratification inevitable within the structure of American society?

7. The past half-century has seen immense changes in a variety of features of black America. Among the more dramatic and visible of these are the fact that blacks have begun to speak boldly to white America, to demand rather than to plead for equality of opportunity in jobs, housing and education. So dramatic have some of these changes been that it is not unrealistic to speak of a black Revolution as having already taken place in this country and as still continuing. Certainly the nation as a whole has been deeply affected by the changes which have taken place in the status of our black citizens.

Using at least the concepts of urbanism and urbanization, social stratification and collective behavior, *explain how and why* these *changes have* occurred. What has happened to the United States in the past fifty years, and to black people in it, which has brought these events about? Why is it happening at this time?

Chapter 6

Deviant Behavior

Deviance as Variance from Norms

In every society there are people and behaviors which are considered socially deviant because they vary in undesirable ways from what the society defines as proper. Deviation, then, implicitly refers to a departure from ideal norms, from what "ought to be." Deviant behavior is activity which differs from what the norms prescribe or prohibit. Deviant people are those who exhibit sufficient amounts of deviant behavior or a few deviant behaviors of such severity that they are seen as being different from other people. Thus, deviation is popularly understood to mean a departure from some standard; that is, deviant behavior is perceived as a failure to observe social norms.

Deviation also is popularly seen as being pathological in character; that is, deviants are supposed to be pathological individuals and deviant behavior is supposed to be either sick or vicious. People usually believe that there is "something wrong" with people who violate popular standards, who do not do what they are supposed to do, who choose to defy conventional norms. To define a behavior or an individual as deviant, then, is to make a moral judgment as well as an empirical one. It is necessary to judge that a norm has been violated and that it was wrong to do so. In both ways the judgment reflects the normative structure of the society.

Despite this popular view of deviance, sociologists have reason to doubt both the pathological character of much deviation and its departure from social norms.[1] One of the problems of understanding deviant behavior, at least in large, complex soci-

---

[1] The belief that deviant behavior is pathological is an old one in Western thought. It accepts a medical-organic analogy of society in which the society is viewed as a living body and normative violation is defined as a sickness which must be cured for the sake of the health of the body politic. The analogy may have been developed to replace an essentially spiritualistic or demonological theory of deviance at a time when the breakdown of the church and the onslaught of science was casting doubt on medieval understanding of human behavior. Needless to say, the medical-organic analogy is a poor one. A society is not an organic system; we have neither a germ theory of deviant behavior nor any medicine with which to "treat" it. This analogy is, however, more humane than the spiritual theory of deviation, for it implies that if a deviant is "sick," he should be treated for his illness, rather than tortured in order to drive out the evil spirits possessing him or burned at the stake as a punishment for having sold his soul to the devil.

eties, is that the society is likely to have more than one set of norms for judging deviation. Probably every society has a popular culture whose norms are known to most members of the society, and the people will more or less conform to many of them. But in heterogeneous societies such as the United States we also find subcultures of region, race, class, occupation, and ethnicity. Such subcultures typically develop some norms of their own which differ from those of the larger society. Thus, what is deviant by the norms of the larger society may be conforming by the norms of the subculture, and vice versa. These norm conflicts are relatively rare only in simple societies.

Another problem in understanding deviation is the distinction made earlier between ideal and statistical norms. In addition to the many normative systems produced by subcultures, complex societies may also have both formal (ideal) and informal (statistical) normative systems within their popular culture. For instance, there is a distinction between kinds of behavior formally required by law and what people actually do (and what the police may ignore). In the United States most drivers violate speed limits occasionally, and many of them do so habitually (though not severely most of the time). In this example the ideal of norm is the legal speed limit, but the statistical norm is the typical behavior. It may be confusing to note that it is the statistical norm rather than the ideal norm which is usually observed by the members of the society and enforced by the police.[2]

In practice there is a range of permissible variation about most norms. Thus, deviation is not just any departure from an ideal norm but rather one which exceeds the amount of permissible variation. Strictly speaking, most people probably deviate from most ideal norms most of the time. As long as they do not depart from them *too far*, they are not perceived as being deviant (different, pathological), because in statistical facts they are

---

[2]   Few of us would expect to receive a traffic ticket for driving thirty-two miles an hour in a thirty-mile-an-hour zone; and if we did, we would be inclined to feel that the arresting officer was being officious, deliberately ignoring the true norms of the case.

not; that is, everyone else behaves the same way. Someone who gets drunk occasionally is not viewed as being an alcoholic; but someone who never violates a speed limit is looked on as being a "nut" (deviant) for observing the norm too rigidly.

Deviance as a Failure of Social Control

In Western societies deviance is popularly understood as resulting from a failure of the mechanisms of socialization and social control. That is, deviants are perceived to be individuals who for some reason are not inhibited by the same considerations that inhibit the rest of us. This understanding is the basis of the American and British penal systems. If people who perform "bad" or socially disapproved actions are punished for them, they will fear the punishment more than they will desire to again commit the prohibited acts. Also, other people will see them as examples and will be deterred from doing the same kinds of things. Originally this theory substituted the contemporary type of prison for torture and capital punishment; it was conceived as a humane reform of Western penal systems. Freud's belief that human behavior is a function of socialization and of a lack of control over elemental processes (the "drives") fits into this theory of punishment. If socialization is adequate, people will conform to the norms of their society; if they do not conform, the social control mechanisms have failed in those particular cases. Deviation is explained by failure in the individual deviant, an inadequacy of his history, psychology, or even constitutional makeup. It can be understood, then, by studying the characteristics of deviants in order to determine "where they went wrong," and it can be deterred by making its costs too high.

Since about the time of the Second World War this theory of deviation and punishment has come under increasing criticism from social scientists. Approximately two centuries of penal treatment of criminals, for example, has failed to greatly alter either the frequency or the nature of crime. The American public is just beginning to understand what sociologists have known for almost fifty years: The prison system, far from deterring crime or rehabilitating criminals, serves as advanced education in criminal activity for most of its inmates. No concrete evidence has yet been developed to support the belief that most types of behavior popularly understood as deviant are much different from other kinds of behavior. Nor is there any evidence that many "deviant" actions are performed by persons who differ in any significant way from the so-called law-abiding (purportedly nondeviant) population. Furthermore, there seems to be no evidence that most people who are defined as deviant have had upbringings significantly different from those of other people. In fact, on most psychological and biological measures, such "deviant" populations as institutionalized criminals or delinquents do not differ for the most part in any important ways from the population beyond their prison walls. A number of the patients in mental hospitals also seem to be no different in important ways from the population of a prison or of a typical town.[3]

The idea, then, that deviant behavior is a characteristic of special kinds of individuals and is itself significantly different from "normal" behavior seems inadequate as a description of the way the world really works. Most people who are considered deviant cannot be distinguished from other people in any way that would explain their behavior. Indeed, much of the behavior popularly called deviant turns out to be pretty much the same as what most people do most of the time anyway. Popular understanding of this, however, has lagged far behind scientific recognition. Only in the last thirty years or so have social scientists even begun to develop new ideas and theories to replace those still enshrined in the law and the public mind.

Let us consider the two propositions on which popular understanding of deviation may be said to rest.

1.   There are two kinds of people who are essentially different from one another, deviants and nondeviants (the "law-

---

[3]   In fact, it is quite probable that significant proportions of the populations of state prisons, state mental hospitals, and, say, local Army posts could be physically exchanged for one another without causing any changes in either the conduct of the three institutions or the behavior outcomes of those switched.

abiding"). If this is true, the only criterion on which the two can be distinguished is that deviants do deviant things; that is, their behavior is different from that of nondeviants. But is this true? Can any reader honestly say he has never broken a law? Stolen something? Violated a no-smoking ordinance? We pointed out earlier that most of us who drive habitually violate the law all the time, that it is the norm to violate some norms. All of us, then, are "deviants" in that we are norm violators; or, to put it another way, norm violation alone and of itself is not what distinguishes deviants from nondeviants or "criminals" from "good people."[4]

2.   There are some kinds of activities which are inherently wrong, improper, or indecent. "Good people" recognize this, abhor such activities, and refuse to engage in them. Deviants, either because they are sick or depraved, may do such things—sometimes even seeking them out.   Again we must ask ourselves if this is really true. When we think about the matter objectively, it is difficult to think of any behavior which is *inherently* antisocial rather than being so defined by the circumstances in which it takes place. Killing is only murder under certain circumstances, and taking what does not belong to you is not necessarily larceny. Many of us take drugs which alter our mental or physiological state, and so common a felony as statutory rape is defined as felonious only when the lady in question is under a certain age. In other words, most of us often engage in specific behaviors which would be defined as deviant *under other circumstances.*

We may conclude that contrary to popular belief and understanding, deviance is a quality inherent in neither behaviors nor persons. In most cases there is nothing peculiar about deviant people or about the "deviant" things they have done. They are

---

[4]   Not all "criminals" are behind bars by any means. See James S. Wallerstein and Clement J. Wyle, "Our Law-Abiding Law-Breakers," *Probation* 25 (March-April 1947); James F. Short, Jr., "A Report on the Incidence of Criminal Behavior, Arrests and Convictions in Selected Groups," *Research Studies of the State College of Washington* 22 (June 1954); and Austin L. Porterfield, "Delinquency and Its Outcome in Court and College," *American Journal of Sociology* 49 (November 1943).

deviance is culture

Merton

Becker

people very much the same as other people, and what they do is not very different from what other people do either. What, then, is an accurate explanation of deviance?

Deviation and Social Structure

As we suggested earlier, social science in recent years has begun to cast doubt upon the propositions underlying the popular understanding of deviation and to develop new theories which seem to fit the observable facts more adequately. These theories explain deviance in the following way.

1. There are circumstances in which the nature of the society itself can generate definite pressures upon individuals or social groups which lead them to nonconforming behavior; that is, there are circumstances in which nonconformity is a reasonable and entirely normal response to the demands of the society.

2. "Deviation" is a characteristic of neither acts nor persons. It is a label which gets applied to some people as the result of a long social transaction. These explanations are partially congruent with one another. The first is offered by Robert K. Merton, a sociologist who attempts to explain why high rates of certain kinds of deviant behavior (for example, crime and suicide) characterize some groups more than others. He seeks to answer the fundamental question: "How does deviant behavior persist in the face of social disapproval?"[5] The second explanation, referred to as labeling theory, is offered by Howard S. Becker, a sociologist who attempts to explain how individuals come to be identified as deviants by the societies in which they live.[6]

Merton's work largely concerns itself with group phenomena, while Becker's work is aimed mainly at individuals. In this they are complementary. Using Merton's theory we can begin to

---

[5]　Robert K. Merton, "Social Structure and Anomie," *Social Theory and Social Structure* (Glencoe: The Free Press, 1949).

[6]　Howard S. Becker, *Outsiders: Studies in the Sociology of Deviance* (New York: The Free Press of Glencoe, 1963).

understand why some social groups have a greater incidence of deviant behavior than others; using Becker's theory we can learn how groups may come to be labeled as deviant in themselves and how some individuals in such groups may not be defined as deviant while others are. The primary difference between the two theories is that Merton accepts the idea that some kinds of behavior really are deviant, even though the individuals engaging in them may be responding positively to social pressure from their culture rather than in an antisocial manner. Becker, on the other hand, questions if there is any such thing as deviant behavior (as distinguished from nondeviant behavior) in the first place, or if deviation is something that is defined after the fact.

Merton's argument is contained in his famous theory of anomie.[7] This theory explains that social structures can sometimes generate pressures on certain individuals or social groups to engage in nonconforming behavior. When this occurs, the individual must violate some norms in order to conform to certain social pressures. If we can locate groups in society which are particularly subject to such pressures, we might expect rates of deviant or nonconforming behavior among them to be relatively high, regardless of the characteristics of the individuals who make up such groups.

Through socialization, all societies teach their members two important particulars of their culture—cultural goals (the things that are worth striving form) and cultural means (the norms which are considered appropriate for seeking and attaining the goals). Under most circumstances, the members of a society are able to use the means they have learned are legitimate in order to attain the ends they have been taught to desire. It is impor-

---

[7] *Anomie* is a term invented by the French sociologist Durkheim. It means literally "normlessness" and is used to describe a mental condition in which the individual is unsure of how he is expected to behave, due to lack of understanding or knowledge of the social rules. Durkheim used the word to explain the relatively higher suicide rates among the widowed and single than among the married and among noncommissioned as opposed to commissioned officers in the army, that is, among people whose bonds holding them to others were, for one reason or another, weak.

tant that this should be true, for a failure to attain the goals we have internalized results in a loss of self-esteem (a lowered judgment of ourselves by ourselves) and a "pain that only human beings can experience."[8] This loss of self-esteem is not only extremely painful but may also be psychologically damaging, and people will do almost anything to avoid it. Most of the time they do not have to do anything. However, there are some individuals and groups who, although they have been taught to seek the same cultural goals as the rest of us and to utilize the same norms in the search, are denied access to the means for their goal attainment. In the United States material success is defined as a cultural goal; and competition is defined as the cultural means to that goal. But there are some groups (for example, black or other nonwhite Americans) whose members are not permitted to compete, or who are permitted to do so only under conditions of considerable disadvantage, although the demand that they be successful is maintained. Using Merton's argument, we would expect higher degrees of deviant behavior among the members of such groups than among members of other groups which had no roadblocks set in their path by the social structure.

Merton proposes five possible combinations of access to or acceptance of means and ends (goals), four of which represent social situations that can produce anomic, or deviant, reactions among persons subjected to them. These reactions may occur when "the system doesn't work," when people, because of their position in society, are denied access either to the means for reward or to the rewards (goals) which their legitimate use of the means ought to bring. They may occur also when the lowered self-esteem experienced as a result of either condition leads these people to socially unacceptable attempts to escape their plight. The five combinations are conformity, innovation, ritual-

---

[8]   I am indebted for the phrase and some of my argument to an excellent social problems textbook which utilizes the Merton theory as its theoretical framework. Although old enough now that some of its illustrations may strike modern students as quaint, it remains, in my opinion, the best social problems text ever written. See Harry C. Bredemeier and Jackson Toby, *Social Problems in America* (New York: John Wiley & Sons, Inc., 1960).

ism, retreatism, and rebellion. With the exception of conformity, all the other combinations are anomic, or deviant, reactions.

The reader might find it easier to comprehend Merton's model for predicting deviant behavior if he observes the following table. The pluses represent acceptance of and access to the cultural phenomenon in question, and the minuses represent rejection and/or lack of access.

Methods of Adaptation To Societal Means-Ends	Culturally Prescribed Means To Social Goals	Culturally Prescribed Goals
Conformity	+	+
Innovation	−	+
Ritualism	+	−
Retreatism	−	−
Rebellion	∓	∓

(handwritten annotations: "what you should be" above "Culturally Prescribed Means"; "what you should strive for" to the right of "Culturally Prescribed Goals")

Conformity.   The individual accepts and internalizes both the cultural goals and the cultural means which he has been taught, and his social position gives him adequate access to both. This is what most people do most of the time.

Innovation.   The individual accepts the cultural goals he has been taught; but because of a social position which denies him access to those means which his society defines as legitimate, he "innovates" (invents new means of attaining the socially desired ends). The most common example of this kind of innovation is crime. In the United States crime can often be explained as a response to excessive cultural emphasis on material success with a corresponding lack of emphasis on the legitimacy of the means used to attain this goal.

Ritualism.   The individual accepts and internalizes both the cultural goals and the means which he has been taught. However, if he fails to attain the goals he has learned to want (perhaps because of inadequate access to the means for their attainment), he psychologically diminishes the importance of attaining the goal and exaggerates the significance of the socially approved means. An example of this is the losing coach who tells his team how important it is that they played fairly while their winning opponents cheated. Another example is the "radical right" in the United States, which seems to be composed mainly of persons who in one way or another have already lost the status game but who make up for it by accentuating one legitimate means to status by preverting patriotism into superpatriotism.[9]

Retreatism.   The individual rejects the claims to legitimacy of both the socially defined means and ends and withdraws from the painful situation entirely. He does this because he has failed to attain the rewards which he has been taught to pursue in order to maintain an adequate self-image. He stops trying to be successful and rejects the value of the goals which success presumably would have offered. The conventional forms of retreatism in American society are alcoholism, suicide, drug addiction, and some forms of mental illness. Retreatism also is a prominent theme in some facets of the contemporary American youth culture. More than the other anomic reactions, retreatism is a response for "losers."

Rebellion.   The individual either accepts the cultural means while rejecting the goals or vice versa. This anomic adaptation is characterized by the individual's attempt to substitute forcefully new means or goals for the societal ones he rejects. Rebellion differs from innovation by virtue of the rebel's attempt to substitute the new goals for the society as well as for himself. When rejecting means rather than goals, it differs from ritualism in that new means for attaining societal goals are again proposed for everyone. Rebellion may result either from lack of access to means or their failure to produce expected rewards, or from the frustration of self-esteem which the latter may create. Familiar

---

[9]   See Ira S. Rohter, "The Righteous Rightists," *Trans*action 4, No. 6 (May 1967): 27-35.

examples of the two types of rebellion are the secession of the southern states, which led to the Civil War (rejection of societal means but acceptance of societal ends) and the new counter culture developing among some segments of American youth (rejection of societal goals but acceptance of conventional means to the attainment of new goals). Examples of this are ecological actions, the return to rural life, and so on.

The key to understanding Merton's views on anomie and how they contradict the idea of deviation as being some form of personal pathology is to remember that in the four anomic adaptations (or reactions) the individuals are behaving as they have been taught by their societies. They are not sinful or weak individuals who choose to deviate. They are, in fact, doing what they have learned they are supposed to do in order to earn the rewards which their society purports to offer its members. But either because their positions in the social structure do not permit them access to the means through which to seek the rewards they have learned to want, or because the means do not in fact guarantee goal attainment, they become frustrated and experience loss of self-esteem. In a final attempt to do and be what they have been taught they must, they engage in what is called deviant behavior. Such behavior is simply an attempt to gain the same self-esteem which others are presumed to have and which the society has made it intolerable to be without. In the case of crime in the United States, material success is the desired goal. Thus, deviant behavior may be seen as an understandable social response on the part of normal people to situations where they cannot do or be what their society has claimed is necessary. It is the behavior of people so thoroughly socialized in the means-ends mechanism of their society that even when the system is out of balance due to an inappropriate assignment of weight on goals or means they are unable to do anything but attempt to work out their destinies and suffer the consequences. As we have seen, such "deviant" responses are particularly prevalent among social groups who are peculiarly subject to societal imbalances—the poor, nonwhite, immigrants, women (under some circumstances), children, and so on.

Becker's work also supports the sociological perception that deviant behavior is the product of social interaction rather than an attribute of deviant persons themselves. As we indicated earlier, Becker has founded a new school of thought on deviant behavior which has come to be known as labeling theory. The basic position from which Becker argues may be seen in the following extract from his work.

> *Social groups create deviance by making the rules whose infraction constitutes deviance,* and by applying the rules to particular people and labeling them as outsiders [deviants]. From this point of view, deviance is *not* a quality of the act the person commits, but rather a consequence of the application by others of rules and sanctions to an "offender." The deviant is one to whom that label has successfully been applied; deviant behavior is behavior that people so label.[10]

If we accept this idea of the nature of deviance, then certain other conclusions must logically follow. The point of the excerpt is that groups make the rules which are used to define deviance for them, but the rules are not enforced universally and identically. Some people are punished for doing something, while others are not punished for doing the same thing; some actions are defined as deviant only because they occur in a particular time, place, or context. What constitutes deviation, then, is something other than particular people or particular behaviors. Deviance is a label, and in order to understand it we must understand the social process through which labels are successfully applied and why and how they are applied to some people and not to others.

Becker points out that if deviance consists of the responses of other people to an act by an individual, then we cannot assume the existence of a homogeneous category of deviant persons. That is, the "deviance" of those who have acquired a particular deviant label is only the response of others to something they did, and their actions may not have been identical or even similar. Not all people who have killed are defined as murderers, and

---

[10]   Becker, p. 9.

not all who have committed the act called murder are known to have done so; some murderers escape the label. As a matter of fact, not only can we not assume that everyone who is labeled as deviant in some particular way has committed the same act in order to get labeled that way, but we cannot even be sure that every "deviant" has committed a "deviant" act at all, since labels are sometimes misapplied.

Then, according to Becker's labeling theory, the key to understanding deviant behavior is to understand that the application of the label "deviant" is simply the last stage of a social transaction between an individual and some social group. In order to learn how and why the label is applied, we must know the "natural history" of the transaction, that is, the series of interactions which resulted in the person being publicly identified as a deviant (nut, fairy, Red, and so on). The rules which govern the interaction between the individual and the social group and which determine whether or not the label will be successfully applied seem reasonably clear.

1. The only thing which we can be sure people who have been labeled deviant share in common is the experience of being so labeled. Beyond that, we cannot be certain. (This is not an attempt to deny that most people convicted of larceny have in all probability stolen something. But so have all of us. The key question is why some thieves become known as criminals and others—the rest of us—do not.)[1 1]

2. This being the case, whether a given act is deviant depends not upon the nature of the act but upon how other people react to it. The degree to which others respond to a given act

---

[11]   I do not mean to imply that all larceny is the same or that most people engage in serious theft throughout their lives. However, it does seem to be a fact (as Porterfield's research on university students and my own questioning of college classes demonstrates) that practically everyone has stolen something at some time in his life, if only pennies from his mother's purse or stamps from his employer. But we do not normally regard ourselves or others as thieves. That is, the act of committing a theft is not what defines a person as a thief. As a matter of fact, a great many so-called law-abiding people habitually engage in various larcenies such as stealing tools, materials, merchandise, or time from an employer, falsifying expense accounts, and shoplifting.

is variable, and a number of factors seem to influence their responses. Among these are the following.

Time.   The same acts may be punished at one time and ignored at others (as in recurrent "law enforcement drives" directed against gambling or prostitution in big cities). Or time itself may be the only variable defining a given act as deviant. The example of statutory rape is particularly instructive. Statutory rape is defined simply as sexual intercourse with a girl who is under "the age of consent" (whatever that may be in a given state). It is independent of the consent or nonconsent of the girl. Similarly, the use of LSD was not illegal anywhere in the United States until about ten years ago. On the day in which the law forbidding it came into effect in a particular state, an act that had the day before been legal became felonious.

Social roles and statuses of the "deviant" and the person or persons supposedly harmed by the "deviant" act.   Whether certain behaviors are defined as deviant is a function of who commits them against whom. In many southern or southwestern towns a Mexican American or a Negro who assaults an Anglo with a knife would be accused of attempted murder or assault with a deadly weapon and would probably be severely punished for the action. The same person attacking a member of his own ethnic group might be defined simply as a participant in a "cutting scrape" and would probably get off with a bash on the head from a policeman's nightstick. Similarly, an attack by a white on a person defined as nonwhite might simply be referred to as a "good old boy who got likkered up too much one night and went out nigger bashin'." Obviously, rules tend to get applied more to some people than to others.[12]

Political influence

[12]   In college towns it is not uncommon for professors who are found driving while intoxicated to be driven home by the police with a quiet—or even humorously condescending—lecture as their total punishment, while students found in the same conditions can expect at least to spend the rest of the night in the drunk tank and might be reported to the school and expelled.

Specific consequences.   Some rules are enforced only when the behavior they forbid has a particular set of consequences and are largely ignored at other times. The conventional rules forbidding premarital sexual relations, for example, are traditionally applied only when the female partner becomes pregnant—and then only against her. Who has ever heard of an unmarried father being expelled from his high school.

Becker summarizes the labeling theory position on the nature of deviance as follows.

> Deviance is not a simple quality, present in some kinds of behavior and absent in others. Rather, it is the product of a process which involves the responses of other people to the behavior. The same behavior may be an infraction of the rules at one time and not at another; may be an infraction when committed by one person, but not when committed by another; some rules are broken with impunity, others are not. In short, whether a given act is deviant or not depends in part on the nature of the act (that is, whether or not it violates some rule) and in part on what other people do about it . . . . we must recognize that we cannot know whether a given act will be categorized as deviant until the response of others has occurred. Deviance is not a quality that lies in behavior itself, but in the interaction between the person who commits an act and those who respond to it.[13]

Deviant Careers

We have explained the contemporary sociological case against conventional ideas about the nature of deviant behavior and of people defined as deviant by the society. In many respects it appears, as Dickens observed so long ago, that "the law [and public understandings us well] is a[n] ass . . ." But that comment does not answer the important analytical question of why certain individuals are identified as deviant while others who

[13]   Becker, p. 14.

perform the same actions are not. Merton's theory explains why some behaviors defined as deviant continue to occur despite public disapproval and why they are more frequent among certain social groups than among others; but it does not explain why some individuals are labeled deviant while others in similar situations are not.

Becker attempts to explain the labeling of individuals through his concept of the deviant career. This concept defines the "natural history" of the social process which results in successful labeling of certain persons as deviant. The idea of "career" is a useful one for this purpose, because it suggests a sequence of steps from one position to another within a social system by a member of that system. It includes such considerations as recruitment and training, socialization and resocialization, occupational subcultures, career contingencies (the factors upon which mobility from one stage to another depend), and so on. Each of these considerations is useful in analyzing the process whereby some people come to be known as deviants.

The first step in the creation of a deviant identity is usually the commission of a nonconforming act—the violation of a norm—occasionally by accident, but usually by intent. But the idea that *intended* nonconformity constitutes a necessary condition for the popular conception of deviance implies that the fundamental difference between the deviant and the nondeviant is *motivation*, that deviants are people who *want to* violate norms. This is a basic assumption of the traditional understanding of deviance and of contemporary law and penology, but it may be entirely erroneous. There is no reason to believe that only those persons who are defined as deviant have ever experienced the desire to commit a deviant act. Appraisal of our own fantasies would reveal that most of us commonly experience impulses to commit assault, larceny, rape, or murder. We should not ask why deviants want to do things which are publicly disapproved, because everyone experiences such impulses. Instead, we should ask why some people *follow through* on their impulses and act them out while others do not.

Becker proposes a partial answer to this question in his concept of "commitment." As they mature, most people experience what might be called a "commitment process," during which they become progressively more committed to conventional behaviors, norms, and institutions. They discover that while at age seventeen they did not need to worry about financial standing, credit rating, or the opinion of the business community, at age thirty-seven, with a mortgage to pay off and children growing up, they do. Maturation in any society may be seen as the development of this increasing series of commitments to a variety of social institutions, organizations, and agencies. Thus, when an individual experiences an impulse to act in a deviant manner (as most of us do with some frequency), he is able to hold it in check by considering what this indulgence might cost him. Most of us, Becker says, have staked too much on being "normal" often to permit ourselves to be swayed by impulses to deviate.

We can understand some deviant behavior, then, by observing that it is expressed by those who have managed to grow up outside the normal commitment process, who never have become implicated in the web of standard relationships, commitments, and conventions. Those who have no reputation to maintain, no job to lose, or, perhaps most importantly, no conventional self-image to uphold, can afford to act in nonconforming ways. Examples of subcultures with values considerably different from those of the main culture include some of the black separatist organizations and carnivals.[14]

Most people, however, make the conventional commitments and remain sensitive to conventional norms and values. They are forced to deal with their own moral codes the first time they engage in deviant behavior; that is, their self-image suffers even if their reputation is unaffected. Typically, people set aside

---

[14]   The carnival, in fact, may represent one of the most deviant of familiar subcultures. As opposed to the circus, which tends to be very conventional, the carnival operates at the margins of the law and normal conventions. Barnum's dictum, "Never give a sucker an even break!" is from the culture of the carnival, not the circus.

their qualms and justify their deviant acts to themselves through what are called "techniques of neutralization."[15] That is, they create psychological rationalizations or justifications for their behavior, or substitute "good reasons" for the real ones, as one psychiatrist has defined it. The function of the technique of neutralization is to make the nonconforming act appear necessary or expedient to the individual. Since he is essentially nondeviant, if he undertakes the pursuit of so-called necessary interests, his deviant act may seem, if not quite proper, at least not clearly improper to him.

Once a deviant act has been committed and rationalized through a successful technique of neutralization, it becomes possible for the behavior to be repeated. For example, a second act of adultery or theft is probably much easier for most people than is the first. Repetition of deviant acts can lead in turn to the development of deviant motives and interests. Becker observes that "many kinds of deviant activity spring from motives which are socially learned. Before engaging in the activity on a more or less regular basis, the person has no notion of the pleasures to be derived from it; he learns these in the course of interaction with more experienced deviants."[16]

Perhaps the most crucial step in the process of creating a deviant "career" is the experience of being caught in a deviant act and publicly labeled as a deviant. This step has a peculiar quality, in that the individual does not choose to take it himself. If he is engaging in deviant behavior, whether he is caught and what happens as a result is largely a matter of others' actions, over which he may have no control whatsoever. (He may, of course, voluntarily label himself through confession of his behavior. Feelings of guilt may even lead people to confess to crimes they did not commit; the police encounter this phenomenon every time there is a spectacular crime, bizarre murder, and so on.) But the public branding of a deviant has pro-

---

[15]   Greshman Sykes and David Matza, "Techniques of Neutralization," *American Sociological Review* 22 (December 1957).

[16]   Becker, p. 30.

found consequences for his future, because it marks a radical alteration in his social identity. Deviation is a matter of status (like sex or race in the United States) around which other roles and behaviors are thought to cluster. For example, if someone is revealed as "queer," it is generally believed that he is therefore untrustworthy concerning national security information. If a man has been in prison, he is henceforth believed to be *generally* dishonest (although check forgers, as a type, are unlikely to be stickup men). In other words, a deviant trait has generalized symbolic value, and people believe that other such traits must be associated with it. For example, long hair on men is associated popularly with a host of deviant traits, such as taking drugs, not having a job, and so on.

This identification of a person as generally rather than specifically deviant has a profound effect upon him. It produces a self-fulfilling prophecy by setting in motion social interactions which act to shape the person in the image which he now publicly bears. The case of the ex-convict is classic. Most men come out of prison on parole. Typically, a condition of parole is that the individual must be self-supporting in "honest work." Equally typically, he is required to inform prospective employers that he is an ex-convict. But these conditions of parole greatly reduce his chances of finding legitimate employment, thus raising the probability that he will have to turn to illegitimate employment once more simply to earn his living. When others treat a person known to have deviated once as if he were continuing to do so, they maximize the probability that he will do so. Treating a person as a deviant deprives him of the means of carrying on ordinary life and encourages him to develop an unconventional life-style.

The final step in the development of a deviant career is movement into a deviant group. Often this move is made because the group offers some knowledge of survival techniques in a hostile world, emotional support, positive reinforcement for the self-image as deviant, and so on. Once an individual has made this move and accepted it, his acceptance itself exercises a powerful effect upon his self-image. It is one thing, for example, for a person to know that he has once committed a homosexual act.

re habilitation

It is quite another for him to acknowledge himself as gay and a member of the gay society. Deviant groups tend to develop self-justifying rationales for their behavior and to form conflict groups with which members may face the world more securely than they might alone. Rewards are offered the new recruit for "coming aboard," and a life-style which permits him to do so with a minimum of effort is made available to him.

We can see from the preceding discussion that contrary to centuries of popular understanding, to conventional law, and to a considerable body of contemporary psychiatry, deviation may be understood as a normal social process in which people pretty much like everyone else, acting in ways not particularly unique, come to have special social identities as a consequence of their relations with others in their society. These identities, as identities, are like conventional roles and statuses which other people share, except that they are defined by others as unconventional.

The purpose of the detailed treatment which deviation has been given in this chapter is multiple. It has sought to establish at least four concepts for the reader's satisfaction.

1. What "everybody knows" about human behavior is not necessarily true; the conventional wisdom of a society is nothing more than conventional.

2. Even very individualistic kinds of behavior have social components and can be subjected usefully to sociological analysis.

3. The individualistic-psychologistic perspective which is so much a part of the cultural understanding and outlook of contemporary Americans is not adequate to explain and understand even rather personal and subjective phenomena.

4. Much human behavior cannot be understood only in terms of motive but must also be analyzed in the light of social process.

Beyond this, we have tried to suggest that a great deal of what we regard as everyday reality is, in fact, a matter of social consensus (agreement among the members of a society) and that the "ultimate reality" of events in society is based on definition. We said much earlier that man is the most symbolic of animals, that he lives his life submerged in a sea of symbols.

Our discussion of deviant behavior illustrates the implications of that truth more clearly than anything we have previously discussed. Finally, it is hoped that consideration of the discussions offered in this chapter will suggest to the student that there is indeed a utility for this special field of study. Deviant behavior has been a matter of interest and concern to human beings at least from the time history was first written and presumably for centuries before men began putting their musings into writing. Our understanding of the law leads us to one perception of deviance; the moral codes of various religions suggest another. But if our purpose is to *understand* our fellow men or to predict their behavior reliably, the examples given in this chapter indicate that sociology has something to offer which more traditional views of man do not. Human society and human social behavior are made up of far more than meets the eye, but the alerted eye can sometimes see beyond what things appear to be and can comprehend them in ways that conventional understandings cannot.

Suggested for Further Reading

Howard S. Becker, *The Other Side*
Howard S. Becker, *Outsiders*
Clifford Beers, *A Mind That Found Itself*
Albert K. Cohen, *Delinquent Boys*
Erving Goffman, *Asylums*
J. B. Martin, *Why Did They Kill?*
Stephen Schafer, *The Victim and His Criminal*
Edwin Scheer, *Crimes Without Victims*
J. H. Skolnick, *Justice Without Trial*
Edwin H. Sutherland, *The Professional Thief*
Edwin H. Sutherland, *White Collar Crime*
Frederic M. Thrasher, *The Gang*
Thorstein Veblen, *The Theory of the Leisure Class*

Topics and Questions for Discussion

1. Deviant behavior may be seen as a reasonable response to perfectly normal social situations. Support this view.

2. Behaviors that are neither immediately dangerous nor forbidden by law may sometimes, nonetheless, be defined as "deviant" by the general public, and treated or reacted to as illegal or immoral. Using some recent example explain (1) why the public may feel that way, and (2) why sociologists may not.

3. Culture and social organization pervade every society (in a sense they *are* society) and are almost invariably taken for granted by the members of a society. When deviations occur, therefore, they are apt to be defined by many people as bizarre, pathological, and perhaps dangerous. More than one sociologist, however, has held that social deviation is normal or natural activity, "an integral part of all healthy societies." As a sociologist, (1) how can you account for (explain) the viewpoint held by "many people?" (2) explain why sociologists may have a different view.

4. Pete Smith is a nice sort of guy. He gets along very well with others and is very receptive to both praise and criticism. He and the people that he associates with may be loosely termed a street gang, nothing heavy like the Black P. Stone Rangers, but still a group of guys that regularly hang around the local gas station. Pete tries to be the best at whatever he does and the thing that he is into now is stripping cars. He and a proficient partner can have everything of value off a parked car in 10 minutes—he's been timed. Because of this skill Pete is very popular with his friends because this activity keeps the gang in coin and provides for the various social functions that they sponsor. One night, however, Pete and his associate were interrupted in their task by the local police. Pete ended up with two years in the state reformatory. Now Pete is both a criminal and deviant, or is he?

5. Some sociologists seem to think that it's society itself that is the cause of deviancy. List a number of arguments that would support this contention. Give an illustration of how a person might conform to those around him and become deviant in the eyes of the larger society and how a person may conform to the goals of the larger society and still be labeled deviant by that society.

6. Socialization seems to be responsible for a person's concept or understanding of himself. If a person considers himself a deviant or a criminal is it the socialization process that is responsible for this view or is it the person himself?

7. Imagine that you are walking through a criminal court building in a large city. Four criminal cases have just been adjourned. The cases are as follows:

Category I: A. Mr. A. has been found guilty of physically assaulting a drunk (breaking his jaw).

The drunk has approached A and his fiancee at a night club and repeatedly asked the fiancee to dance, using abusive language. Mr. A is 20 years old, just out of the Army, and has never appeared in court before.

B. Mr. B has been found guilty of forgery, with more than 100 forged checks attributed to him.

Mr. B is a smartly dressed, young-executive type who has one previous forgery conviction.

Category II: C. C has been convicted on a narcotics charge, having been arrested for the possession of heroin.

C attends an upper class high school, has a stable family life, his father being an electronics engineer and his mother a high school teacher. He is apparently addicted to the drug.

D. D has been convicted for the second time on a charge of prostitution.

D is 25 years old, and apparently has supported herself through prostitution since she was sixteen. She feels that what she does is "nothing" compared to what other people do.

Each of these cases can be understood in a number of different ways. Analyze the cases from a sociological perspective, utilizing *theories of deviance*, as well as your understanding of the process of *socialization*, the formation of *subcultures*, and the development of *"self."*

Chapter 7

More Ways of Thinking Sociologically

Models and Theories

In Chapter 1 we discussed sociological ways of thinking, and in Chapters 2 through 6 we discussed some sociological concepts. In this chapter we will return to the theme developed in Chapter 1, concentrating not upon ideas as such but on ways of thinking about ideas, ways which are not peculiar to sociology but which are characteristic of scientific method. We will explain the use of *models* and *theories* as tools for thinking about the world, and we will discuss the concept of *functionalism*.

A scientific model is a verbal, mathematical, or graphical representation of an idea or of some facet of the world. It is an artificial construct designed around the logic of some argument, hypothesis, or statement. For example, in dealing with social stratification, we presented a four class model of social stratification based on Marx's work. That description of the way the world is presumed to work can be represented diagramatically in a conventional class pyramid.

This model is a graphic representation of the way in which an actual class structure exists. It suggests that two kinds of social relationships, here shown geometrically, operate "out there" in the world. The vertical dimension of the diagram shows four definable social classes in their dominant-subordinate relationships. That is, the more powerful classes are positioned above the less powerful classes in the pyramid. The slope and width of the pyramid and the relative areas of the four sections within it suggest the proportions of people in each class relative to the other classes. To the degree that the drawing is accurate and the model does represent social reality, we can learn what to expect in the world by analyzing the relationships shown in it. Thus, the model is a representation, a construct of reality. It represents only two or three possible dimensions of the myriad relationships between social classes, but it enables us to focus on those two or three in order to understand them.

Model making has two functions.

1. By using models we can study reality in miniature (at least to the degree that the model approximates the world). This is especially useful when it is inconvenient or impossible to perform the real operations of study. For example, we can reproduce some of the conditions of the Antarctic in the laboratory, a method of study which is cheaper and more comfortable than going there. Also, while it is possible and sometimes desirable to fly aircraft into hurricanes to study them, it is also cheaper and less dangerous (for some purposes) to reproduce winds of hurricane velocity in man-made wind tunnels. Similarly, we can reproduce marital conflicts to some extent by the use of role-playing in small groups.

2. We can manipulate certain facets of a model in order to see what effect changes would have in the real world. For example, an engineering laboratory could test physical materials to the point of destruction, and a sociologist could statistically manipulate birth rates to determine the possible effects of perfect contraception.

Basically, there are two kinds of models—reality models and ideal or hypothetical models. Reality models are constructed to represent the world as accurately as possible, at least from some specific framework or perspective. Their function is to say, "This is the way the world looks when we observe it according to certain rules or when we regard only certain dimensions of it." (The class pyramid described earlier is a Marxian reality model.) The ideal or hypothetical model is constructed to show how the world would look or act if certain untrue or unknown conditions were actually true. The pure vacuum of physics is a hypothetical model, as is the economically rational man of classical economics. In either case the function of the model is to answer the question, "What would happen if . . . " where the

"if" involves looking only at certain aspec.
understand it or manipulating this reality to pro.
thetical state for our inspection.

The term *scientific theory* is not well understood; indeed, many social scientists misuse it frequently by substituting it for hypothesis (a proposition about a possible state of affairs, formulated in order to be tested through observation). Thus, the famous Sutherland "theory" of differential association to explain criminal behavior is in fact the hypothesis that people learn to be criminal through socialization in a deviant subculture. *Theory* refers to a body of assumptions, observations, tested propositions, and laws. It is a comprehensive body of universal generalizations based on observations, deductions, and inferences about how the world works; these generalizations are tied together into an integrated whole for the purpose of explanation. Theories are not developed to explain specific events; instead, events (wars, robberies, marriages, and so on) are considered to be examples of the matter to which theory is applied. The purpose of theory is explanation. Models are addressed to the question, "What is the nature of the world?" Theories are addressed to the question, "Why does it work that way?"

Scientific theory is useful because it performs a number of functions which enable the scientist to do his work with more efficiency and accuracy and with less wasted motion and duplication of effort than would otherwise be possible. Popular contempt for the "merely theoretical" reflects the general misunderstanding of the word *theory*, in this case likening it to *speculative* or *hypothetical*. In science, theory is all; reliable explanation, as represented in theory, is what science is about. Following are the functions of scientific theory.

1. Definition of problems. A theory about some aspect of how the world works tells us what we need to know to test it, to push our understanding farther, to explore our confusions, and so on. It poses the questions to be answered by research.

2. Suggestion of hypotheses for exploration of such problems. Theory not only poses problems for us to solve but suggests avenues which may be useful in their exploration. If a given state of affairs is seen to be problematic, then the knowledge already available in the area and the general explanation in the theory are likely to suggest specific propositions which ought to hold true if the theory is accurate. These propositions can then be specifically tested through observation.

3. Direction of investigation by suggesting kinds of data needed to test hypotheses. Once specific hypotheses have been inferred or deduced, the theory can dictate the kinds of data needed to test them. Thus, the theory can be seen as a set of limits within which the test must take place. Only certain data will be seen to fit logically within those limits, and this will narrow choices considerably.

4. Suggestion of methods for evaluating data. Once the data demanded by the theory for testing the hypotheses have been gathered, they must be subjected to some kind of analysis in order to determine whether the observed facts constitute support for the hypotheses. Some forms of analysis will constitute an adequate test, while others will not. The nature of the theory and the service to which the conclusion will be put usually demonstrate what will or will not be an adequate test.

5. Imposition of meaning on findings, if any. Ideally, the investigator knows before he sets out to gather data what it will mean if his hypotheses are supported or not. If the study has been sufficiently rigorous, the meaning of the findings will have been determined ahead of time by the theoretical structure. That is, the "explanation" to which the research has been directed should have been predictable, at least under some conditions of outcome. ("If the hypotheses are supported by the data, then we will have shown . . . ") The *meaning* of the data, then, arises out of the formal structure of the logical process through which the entire investigation has passed; the meaning has been a foregone conclusion if the theoretically expected result is found. What the actual investigation determines is not the meaning of that result but whether the theory has been applicable to the particular case under consideration. (Theory itself is a logical structure. It is never tested directly; only its applications are subject to observation.)

These waters may appear somewhat murky. To clarify the use of models and theories in social science and in analyzing the social world, it may be useful to offer an illustration from a classic sociological research study of social class.

Using a Model to Test the Theory of Social Class

Marx's theory of social class generally perceived societies as being divided into economic strata, or layers, of wealth, determined by "relation to the means of production." Marx believed that membership in these strata influences or determines life chances and that the upper strata exploit the lower, or at least have a competitive advantage over them in securing economic rewards and favorable life chances. One way of testing this theory would be to examine members of different economic classes (as defined by their "relation to the means of production") to see whether in fact their life chances differ and, if so, whether those of the upper strata appear superior to those of the lower. Data in support of these hypotheses would not *prove* the theory in any absolute sense but would constitute support for it. Data contradicting or failing to support the hypotheses would cast doubt on the accuracy of the theory. If our general understanding of the way class operates is correct (and the general understanding is a modification of the Marxian one), then such hypotheses ought to be supported by observation most of the time; otherwise there should be clear special cases or intervening factors to explain why they are not supported. A study of social class and mental illness by August Hollingshead and Frederick Redlich has become classic in sociology.[1] This study constitutes an example of theory testing.

---

[1] August B. Hollingshead and Frederick C. Redlich, "Social Stratification and Psychiatric Disorders, "*American Sociological Review* 18 (April 1953).

Although not devised specifically to test Marxian theory, the argument of the Hollingshead and Redlich study is that the general theory of social class holds that class influences life chances, perhaps particularly the life chances associated with economic factors. It also has been known for a long time that the functional mental illnesses are an outcome of life experience,[2] and that social environment is connected with mental illness in ways not yet clearly understood. The authors decided to examine the actual experience with mental illness of large numbers of people. They believed that if they could show that the chance of becoming mentally ill is not randomly distributed but rather is associated with particular social classes, then our understanding of mental illness would be enlarged and the accepted theory of social class would be supported. Their proposed test was a simple one, based on a "no difference" model; that is, their starting point was that there is no difference between the chance of lower class people and upper class people becoming mentally ill. The authors studied the psychiatric records of treatment facilities in the city of New Haven, Connecticut in order to obtain a complete listing of persons within the city who had been diagnosed as suffering from mental illness in a particular time period. Using a simple five class model of social stratification (based on amount of wealth and the way it was procured, location and kind of residence, appearance in the New Haven *Social Directory*, occupation and education, and so on) they classified the residents of the city, including diagnosed patients. Then they applied the no difference test, which held that if mental illness has no relation to social class (is not a life chance influenced by class), there should be no differences

---

[2] It is conventional to distinguish two varieties of "mental illness"—functional and organic. The organic disorders stem from disease or trauma in the body, such as deterioration of the central nervous system from paralysis, damage as a result of blows, and so on. The functional disorders, on the other hand, have no apparent organic cause; they seem to be related to the patient's functioning in life, the result of his psychological adjustments to stress. By definition, all neuroses are functional, and most of the more common psychoses are believed at least to have functional components. A few of these common psychoses are paranoia, manic-depressive psychosis, and some varieties of schizophrenia.

among the classes in terms of (1) frequency of diagnosed mental illness, (2) types of mental illness, or (3) quality and availability of treatment. Their study showed that the no difference model failed in each test; that is, mental illness is not randomly distributed in the population, and the types of illnesses and the ways in which they are treated are strongly associated with social class position.

For our purposes we need not reproduce the details of the Hollingshead and Redlich study. In that research, the core of the argument was tested by three sets of statistical tables which compared (1) the distributions of the normal and psychiatric (diagnosed) populations among the social classes, (2) the distribution of kinds of mental illness among the classes, and (3) the nature of treatment given among the classes. In each instance, the authors discovered that mental illness was not equally distributed among the classes. Specifically, they found that the higher the social class, the lower the frequency of mental illness; the lower the social class, the greater the frequency of *severe* mental illness; the higher the class, the greater the likelihood that high quality treatment would be given; and the lower the class, the greater the likelihood that no treatment would be given. Thus, the hypothesis that mental illness and its treatment is a life chance related to social class was entirely supported. The support for this hypothesis constitutes further support for the general theory of social class which has been described.

We have discussed this study because it is an excellent illustration of the use and interaction of models and theories in scientific investigation. The study used a reality model (the description of social class) to test an hypothesis (class standing is unrelated to life chances) in ways derived from theory. The theory of class as an economic factor determined by occupation, wealth, and so on and having greater effect upon life opportunities was used to:

(1)   define the problem to be studied (is class associated with mental illnesses and its treatments?);

(2)   suggest the hypothesis to be tested (that class is not associated with specific mental illnesses and treatment);

(3)   suggest the kind of data which would serve to test the

hypotheses (if class could be shown to be related to so apparently uneconomic a phenomenon as mental illness, then the idea that it influences life chances would be strongly supported);

(4) impose meaning on the findings once they were seen to contradict the test hypotheses.

Of the five uses of theory described earlier, only number 4 (the methods selected for evaluating data) was not specifically determined by the theory in use in this case, except to the extent that the selection of the test hypotheses demanded a demonstration of difference among the classes for the theory of social class to be supported (and there are only a limited number of statistical tests appropriate to such demonstration).

In summary, scientific investigation is, above all, a logical process which has as its ultimate aim the production of reliable general information. Models and theories are useful because they map out the logic of inquiries so as to maximize the power of the conclusions to be drawn from them, and they keep thought processes and research efforts orderly, thus making possible the continual integration of systematic discoveries which is the essence of that way of thinking called science. The social sciences do not have either the precision or the rigor of the natural sciences, but they share their logic to some degree, and they pursue the same goals—the development of reliable systematized information about the world and man's place in it. The organization of the social sciences through the use of such logical tools as models and theories is an ongoing effort.

Functionalism

Another way of thinking which has proved immensely useful to the sociologist is called *functionalism*. The functional viewpoint is strongly influenced by evolutionary thought; it is used in biology, anthropology, economics, clinical psychology, and even in fields that are distant from the social sciences, such as architecture. Functionalism is a way of assigning meaning to things according to what effects they produce. Thus, we could say that a bird has wings in order to fly; the meaning of the wing structure is that it permits or produces the function of flight. It seems absurd to make such an assertion, since it is obvious that birds fly because they have wings; if they did not have wings, they could not fly. But this is a *structural* interpretation rather than a functional one because it is focused on the wing rather than the activity of flight. If we look at the evolution of the bird and the logic of the theory of evolution, we find that it is perfectly reasonable to say that birds have wings in order to fly. We can presume that the ancestors of birds had very poorly developed wing structures. But we can also presume (as did Darwin) that individual members whose wing structures were slightly more efficient would have found the superior structure an aid to their survival. Having better use of their wing structures, they would have lived longer and probably bred more frequently, thus returning to the gene pool of their kind the genes for the more efficient wing which they possessed. As this process continued through millenia, the wing would have been further developed, as a function or consequence of flight itself. The ability to fly better than others of his type would enable the better constructed creature to survive and over time to further develop the structure which made his survival possible. Thus, it makes evolutionary sense to say that it was the function of flight which developed the structure of the wing, or that birds have wings in order to fly.

In the same way, functionalism in architecture is a way of thinking which suggests that the purpose of a building's structure is to facilitate the activity or function for which it is being designed. Thus, the function which the building will perform is permitted to determine its structure. Theaters are not built like football stadiums, and classrooms are currently being designed to further the functions of teaching and learning rather than inhibit them (as they did in the past).[3] Although functionalism originated in biology, it now characterizes many other intellec-

---

3   If we agree that the functions of an airline terminal are both the movement and temporary storage of persons, then perhaps no better example of functional architecture exists in the United States than the TWA terminal at John F. Kennedy Airport in New York.

tual endeavors. It is probably best known to the public as the basis for the whole logic of psychotherapy. That is, even the most bizarre behaviors of mentally ill people have some purpose or function or provide some service for them. If the therapist can discover through analysis what that service is, he can begin to understand the nature of the patient's problem.[4]

Characteristics of the Functional Orientation

Functionalism is distinguished from other intellectual orientations by certain characteristic concerns and by the logic of its argument. Its primary concern is to explore behavior, relations, and activities of structures rather than their nature, substance, or properties. Functionalism emphasizes the ties between events as the basis for the meaning of the events themselves. Thus, the functional significance of the bird's wing is not only that it permits flight but also that it has developed out of flight. One of the functions wings have performed for birds has been the development and survival of the creature itself.

A second characteristic concern of functionalism is the understanding that physical or social *structures* are properties of the activities or relations with which they are involved. The structure of the bird's wing is a property of the activity of flight. That is its meaning, and only in that way can the wing be

---

[4]   The reader may be interested in undertaking the following psychological inquiry. I commonly ask students in my classes if they habitually reopen the letter slide of a mailbox in order to make sure that a letter just mailed has, indeed, fallen all the way into the box. As a rule, overwhelming majorities of these college students report that they habitually make such a double check. I then ask how many of them ever have actually found their letter sticking to the slide. Typically, only a tiny percentage admit they have had such an experience. Why, then, do so many of us—the author included—persist in a behavior which is, in fact, irrational, in that the purpose for which we undertake it is to guard against an extremely unusual (and hardly important) contingency? What function or service does the act really perform for us, if indeed it is not related to the reason we tell ourselves it is? According to the two psychiatrists I questioned, the function of a mailbox double-checking, door lock double-checking, and so on is the relief of mild and normal common anxiety. We are not really worried about the letter or the door but just worried in general, and "making sure" helps us relieve our general anxiety.

fully understood. Similarly, the social structure (or table of organization) of an airborne unit as distinguished from a normal infantry organization must be understood as a property of the specific activity for which such a unit is designed, the activity of engaging in combat through being parachuted into battle. Thus, from the functional viewpoint, structures are properties of activities or relationships.

Probably the best definition of *social function* is that it is an activity determined (created or demanded) by the social system in which it occurs and having some role in the perpetuation of that system. That is, social function is a system-determined and system-maintaining activity. (The evolutionary development of the bird's wing is analogous.) Many customs or habitual ways of doing things are examples of social function. The conventional rules of the road for automobile drivers are perhaps a readily understandable one. Automobiles exist in many cultures; they are driven on either the right or the left side of the road, depending on the customs of the particular culture. Wherever autos exist in significant numbers, they must be driven on only one side of the road; otherwise, the resulting traffic jams would be monumental and would make driving impossible. The choice of which side of the road to drive on is a matter of historical accident in any given society. But the need for uniformity in this aspect of driving is unquestionable. The particular custom adopted, then, is both system-determined and system-maintained.

In this understanding of social function some assumptions have been made about the nature of human societies and about the best ways of studying them. Indeed, one of these assumptions involves the purpose of study itself. We observe social phenomena in order to understand them, to comprehend them emotionally and identify with them personally, as well as to know them through the more directly scientific activities of measurement and description. Another assumption is that social life occurs in closed systems of interaction, where the parts "fit together" and are related to one another. This implies a third assumption, that the meaning of any one event or relationship within such a system can be fully comprehended only in terms of its relations with other events or relations.[5] A fourth assumption is that full comprehension of the meaning of an event occurs only when the event has been explained as being both determined by the system in which it occurs (the heart makes the blood circulate by pumping it through the body) and contributing to the perpetuation or survival of that system (the circulation of the blood permits nutrients to reach cells and wastes to be removed, both of which are necessary functions for survival). Events which are socially functional, then, are both system-created and system-maintaining; the society creates them, and they perform services which are essential to the maintenance of the society. A fifth and final assumption of the functionalist viewpoint is that much, if not all, social behavior is functional, that part of its purpose is the perpetuation of the social system within which it occurs.

It is important to understand that we have been discussing only assumptions. When viewing things from a functional perspective we adopt these assumptions about the nature of social reality. *But they are not statements of fact about the world or how it works; they are simply a basis for defining or interpreting facts.* We take them for granted and use them as rules for interpreting our observations. Thus, using the last assumption as an example, when we examine a social event, we assume that it has some function or purpose for the society, and we set out to determine what it might be. From a functional perspective we never question *whether* a routine social event may occur without serving some societal purpose. It is important that we understand this point, because if we assume that an event has some social function and seek to discover it, we almost invar-

---

[5] "System" is a medical concept readily understood through an organic analogy. The human body can be viewed as a total interactive system. Within that system there are subsystems, each of which can be regarded as relatively independent for analytical purposes. (The subsystem for circulation of the blood, for example, is analytically separable from the digestive subsystem.) Within any system or subsystem the function of a particular structure or relation (such as the heart or the relation of veins to arteries can be comprehended only in relation to other structures (organs) or relations (functions).

ably succeed in doing so. That is, *some* function reasonably may be attributed to almost any event. The question of *whether* an event serves a function is much harder to answer. It demands a kind of evidence which is sometimes difficult to establish.[6] But the value of the functional position is in the kinds of hypotheses generated by acceptance of its assumptions. By using these assumptions, we are able to discover things about the world, or possible explanations for events in the world, which might be impossible to generate otherwise.

Probably the most controversial of the five assumptions is that of social behavior being functional. *It demands a presumption about facts which is incapable of denial.* (For example, how is one to prove that the buttons on a coat sleeve have *no* purpose or meaning of any kind?) But this assumption is crucial to the functional position, and it can be made more explicit if we understand the logic of the argument underlying it. Anything in a society which is common or customary *must be* useful to the society or it would not be a standard practice there. The fact that a culture item or practice exists over time is "proof" that it has a purpose. Otherwise it would die out.[7] But even activities or items which serve useful purposes for the society as a whole may nonetheless have negative consequences for individuals or for groups within the society. When this occurs, the negative result is called a "dysfunction." The widespread ostracism of "hippies" that is practiced in the American culture may have distinct positive values for the society as a whole. It may reaffirm common values, provide scapegoats for everything from inflation to the conflict in Indochina, and so on. But this

---

[6]   The row of buttons on the outside cuff of a man's coat sleeve is an instructive example. The buttons serve no apparent purpose. They are not even decorative, since they are normally the same color as the coat material and are thus difficult to discern. We assume, however, that since it is customary to have such buttons on the sleeve, there must be a reason for them. This assumption generates a variety of hypotheses (decoration, maintenance of tradition, support of the button industry, and so on).

[7]   This is, of course, a circular argument, not a statement of fact; but it is a way of understanding facts.

ostracism tends to become somewhat painful (dysfunctional) for the scapegoats, who are, by and large, relatively harmless people. It is difficult to understand rationally why a group of young people retiring to a remote rural area to practice neolithic agriculture are perceived as being dangerous to the welfare of the country because they let their hair grow and occasionally sleep with one another. But the obvious value of hippie-hatred for thousand of Americans can hardly be denied.

Manifest and Latent Functions

We must distinguish between two different ways of interpreting social events or behavior as functional, because the distinction is a powerful tool for analysis. *Manifest functions* involve the motivation for or intended consequences of social acts. They are different from *latent functions*, which involve the actual or objective consequences of social acts. Our aims and our results sometimes differ. This means that the actual effects of social behavior sometimes differ from the effects we ostensibly intend to achieve by our behavior. From the functionalist perspective, the *real* purpose of an action (or behavior) may be the unintended (and sometimes unknown) effect of that action, regardless of why the acting person or group thinks they are performing the action. The manifest function of an action or behavior is its intended consequence, the result which it is intended to produce. When results in addition to those intended actually follow, the unintended additional consequences of the behavior are called latent functions—if they can be shown to serve some purpose for the system which created them. In individuals the search for latent functions is a significant part of clinical psychological inquiry; among groups functional interpretations can expose aspects of reality otherwise undiscoverable.

The principal purpose for the latent-manifest distinction in functionalism is that of allowing the observer to look beneath the surface of conscious intentions for behavior and sometimes to find out why things happen with even apparently irrational social phenomena. (*Irrational* in this sense simply means "incapable of accomplishing the stated end.") Looking for latent functions in behavior which apparently cannot accomplish what it is supposed to accomplish may expose the real reasons for the behavior in question. The basic argument for the concept of latent functioning, then, is simply that when persistent or customary behavior cannot be seen to accomplish that which it is purported to do, the observer must examine its consequences to determine what it *is* doing in order to understand why it continues. In psychotherapy the analyst undertakes this examination in order to understand the nature of his patient's problems. In sociology customs or conventional behavior are examined in order to gain insights into the operation of the social order. Durkheim's conceptions of the functions of religion in society (*The Elementary Forms of the Religious Life*) are an excellent example.

The import of this argument is that both individual and social actions may be undertaken for reasons of which the actors are unaware (even though their actions produce the results which are the real reasons for which the actions are undertaken). We saw a simple example of this earlier in regard to the letter mailing behavior of individual people. Although we tell ourselves that we are checking the slide on the letter box in order to insure that our letter has indeed dropped down, the fact is that mailed letters rarely stick to the slides, which suggests that our checking serves another purpose, probably that of relieving generalized anxiety. Although we may be aware of how this logic operates on an individual level, we are less familiar with the concept of latent social functions for collective behavior; yet, a very persuasive case can be made for the existence of such a concept. An example from the author's personal experience may serve to make this point.

Years ago, while at a military station in the state of Mississippi, I observed a series of simple social actions. When I reflected on these actions many years later, I realized that they exposed in detail the social function of the physical segregation of the races as it was then practiced in the South. I was sitting on a railway station platform in a small Mississippi town, killing a two or three hour wait between trains. The station was built to conform with common architectural practice in the area. It had two waiting rooms labeled "white" and "colored," each with its own open platform area, connected by the station-master's office and ticket booth, which served both rooms. On the outside wall of the stationmaster's office, between the two platforms, were two wall-mounted drinking fountains, side by side, with the small enameled signs of "white" and "colored" hanging on hooks above them. I noted almost immediately up-on sitting down that there were no pipes beneath the "colored" drinking fountain; it was inoperable. I knew from having tried it that the "white" fountain was in working order.

As a northerner in the South for the first time, this state of affairs confirmed my every prejudice concerning the lot of the black man in Mississippi and the petty meanness of the southern white man. One can imagine my confusion when perhaps half an hour after I had arrived, I observed the white stationmaster leave his office, walk to the drinking fountains, and switch the signs above them! In the next few hours this performance was repeated about every thirty minutes, so that the one operable drinking fountain was "white" for about half of each hour and "colored" for the other half.

I am not ashamed to admit that it took me many years and considerable sociological training to fully understand the stationmaster's action. For was not the purpose of segregated eating, drinking, and toilet facilities in this country the physical separation of the races, based on the rationalization that blacks were more liable to disease, less sanitary, and so on? And was not the stationmaster risking his job, if not worse, by defying those beliefs and making it possible for members of both races to drink from the same fountain? The answer to both questions is, of course, no. Observation of the southern caste system, even in its pristine purity (or impurity) of seventy years ago, shows that there was no objection even to very intimate physical association between the races (as witnessed in wet-nursing and other services performed by blacks) so long as the black partner to the interaction was clearly labeled as inferior.

Thus, the latent social function of physical segregation was not the prevention of close physical proximity or of disease transmission; instead it was the prevention of simultaneous access, which would imply competition on more or less equal grounds and which might allow the possibility of black success at the expense of white success. The purpose of having two drinking fountains side by side was not to prevent members of the different races from using the same fountain but to prevent them from attempting to do so at the same time, which might involve a white having to wait for a black. The Mississippi stationmaster clearly understood that principle, even though he probably could not have articulated it and, in fact, probably was unaware of it in any conscious sense.

This observation of the social function of segregation seems to hold true for other areas of southern life. An obvious illustration is found in the differential nature of segregation at indoor movie theaters and drive-in movie theaters. A few years after the above-mentioned events in Mississippi, I was once more stationed in the South (this time in Alabama) and was once more fascinated by what appeared to me a curious variation in the local folkways regarding race. It was alleged that segregation had to be maintained in the interests of health and sanitation of whites, and therefore indoor theaters were rigorously partitioned off into two separate seating areas. Outdoor theaters, however, while they maintained separate ticket booths and entrances, allowed people to park wherever they wanted to once inside the fence. At the time, this practice simply seemed to me another example of southern madness concerning race. I now see it as similar to the drinking fountain episode. That is, the function of segregation was to prevent direct personal competitive confrontation in which whites might lose to blacks. At drinking fountains and in indoor theaters, in places where face-to-face confrontation might occur, the races were physically segregated, but at outdoor movies, where people are isolated, enclosed, and packaged in their cars, no such provisions were necessary. The "drive-in" character of the theaters provided the required physical segregation.

By using the distinction between latent and manifest functions for social behavior, we are able to extend our attention beyond the matter of whether a given act fulfills its avowed purpose, and we are able to discover "purposes" for social behavior of which even the participants may be entirely unaware. This is particularly valuable when some common social practice seems incapable of accomplishing the end which its participants claim to want. When such actions occur, the sociologist is invited by his functional framework to ask what the actions do in fact accomplish to make it worthwhile for the participants to continue engaging in them. Obviously, the answers to such questions are always hypothetical. As in the two racial examples, support must depend upon the formulation of further tests and the gathering of further observations. Functionalism as a means for generating hypotheses has no equal; it enables us to develop tentative explanations of things which would otherwise be impossible. But as we noted earlier, the logic of functionalism is essentially circular. While functional hypotheses can be illustrated and supported by gathering further observations, they can never be proven.[8]

Summary

In this chapter we have been concerned primarily with two special devices for sociological ways of thinking rather than with the content of such thought. We have discussed the use of models and theories in extending our understanding and in enlarging and strengthening the basis of our knowledge. We have used functionalism to derive ideas, hypotheses, or explanations about events often unknown to the participants. Neither of these methods of thinking about the world is peculiar to sociology, but functionalism in particular has gained a wide acceptance in that field.[9]

---

[8]   In this respect, functionalism suffers from the dilemma of induction. No generalization based on anything less than all cases can ever be proven absolutely. Functionalism has been particularly susceptible to criticism, however, because few functional explanations are subjected to the test of further observation by those who expound them.

[9]   Indeed, a former president of the American Sociological Association, in his presidential address to that body, suggested that for all the criticisms of the position, sociological thought and functional understandings were one and inseparable. See Kingsley Davis, "The Myth of Functional Analysis as a Special Method in Sociology and Anthropology," *American Sociological Review* 24 December 1959).

What must be emphasized is that the nature of the questions we ask about the world determines the nature of the answers we will receive. Sociology, like the other disciplines, has a special set of questions which are characterized by particular ways of thinking. Although functionalism is only one of several, it has had immense influence upon the field. Sociology cannot be adequately comprehended without an understanding of it. Equally indispensable are models and theories for ordering our thought and letting us know how well we can know what we think we know.

Suggested for Further Reading

Daniel Bell, (ed), *The Radical Right*
Lewis Coser, *Functions of Social Conflict*
E. Durkheim, *The Division of Labor in Society*
Max Weber, *The Protestant Ethic and the Spirit of Capitalism*
Max Weber, *The Theory of Social and Economic Organization*
Norbert Wiener, *The Human Use of Human Beings*

Topics and Questions for Discussion

1. Walter Bagehott, a 19th century English author-statesman-journalist, once observed that among all peoples or cultures virtues are behaviors which are supportive of the cohesion of the social group while vices or sins are behaviors which are destructive to its cohesion or integrity. He was correct. Why?

2. In early American maritime history there were at least two cases in which the drifting survivors of disasters at sea killed one of their number in order to eat him, and thereby were enabled to endure until rescue. In both of these instances the cannibalistic seamen were tried for murder when it was discovered what they had done, but in one case the survivors were acquitted while in another they were convicted and hanged. Defend *both* decisions sociologically from the perspective of the functions of law or morality for the society as a whole (i.e., argue first one side of the case, then the other from the same sociological perspective).

Chapter 8

Using Sociology

Introduction

The preface to this book affirmed that sociology is relevant because it enables us to comprehend the nature of the world in which we live and because it allows us a possibility of control over events which would otherwise control us. Earlier chapters attempted to explain some simple conceptual tools for analyzing the social world in which we are immersed. In this chapter we will describe a currently problematic social reality, and offer some analysis of the social and demographic conditions which have interacted to produce the problem situation. As we will see, sociology is useful in defining the nature of the problem to be addressed; that problem is the current condition of the American city.

It is generally agreed that the cities of the United States are suffering from physical deterioration, financial anemia, political difficulties in governance, and severe reduction in the quality of life possible in them. In other words, the cities are becoming unlivable. It would be foolish to pretend that sociology offers an easy solution to the problems of cities. The dilemmas and paradoxes which beset the large American city are so many, of such long development, and of such complex interconnection that volumes have been written just attempting to describe them. But sociological analysis of the problems can contribute to their understanding and solution, at least to the degree that it exposes their dimensions and the factors affecting them.

To begin the analysis we will examine some of the social phenomena which have contributed to the present urban condition. As a result of historical social forces the character of the United States has changed radically and fundamentally during the two hundred years of its existence. We began as an agricultural and seafaring nation with an essentially rural population. We have become an industrial nation with an essentially urban population. The city has become the dominant characteristic of American life. But the contemporary city did not spring into being full-grown; it, too, is the product of changing social forces. Chief among these have been three great migrations which shaped the city of today and deeply influenced its character. They are (1) the continuing migration of rural people to urban places, (2) the migration of black people from the rural South to the cities of the North, Midwest, and West, and (3) the migration of the urban middle class from the central city to the suburbs. Influenced by the characteristics of the migrants and the times in which they moved, and interacting with one another, each migration has worked to shape the city into what we see today.

Earlier chapters of the book have explored five fundamental sociological concepts (culture, socialization, social organization, social stratification, and deviance) and something of the nature of sociological thought. In this chapter, we will not attempt to show precisely how each of these concepts can be used to understand what is happening to the city. But our analysis of the nature of contemporary urban problems will utilize each of these concepts in many ways.. For example, only by understanding the social nature of deviant behavior can we understand the persistent nature of much urban crime and disorganization. Similarly, it is impossible to understand the effects of the black migration on the city without comprehension of the caste-like character of American race relations and the class subcultures of black migrants and the urban middle class.

The Scope of the City

In the past hundred years the United States has become an urban nation, in a sense that is probably unknown elsewhere. Indeed, we could paraphrase a recent sociological title and call it "The First Urban Nation." Unquestionably, vast expanses of empty and underdeveloped wasteland remain in the continental United States (such as parts of the Southwest where only red men have lived or great areas of northern Minnesota which are accessible only by canoe or aircraft). But in a cultural sense the United States is an urban nation; its people are city people. The author once saw a Basque sheepherder's wagon in a roadless mountain valley of Colorado, miles from any town, with a television antenna on its roof. The lonely man in that wagon watched the same programs from the same cities as did the residents of Los Angeles, New York City, and Lincoln, Nebraska.

While the various localities in the United States retain control over their school systems, all American children are schooled according to similar curricula, designed by state school authorities in order to meet national standards. They also read similar textbooks and watch similar educational films, all originating in a handful of cities and developed and produced by small numbers of essentially urban people—professors, artists, scientists, publishers, and so on. In these and a thousand other ways, then, the nation's culture has been homogenized, and now it is largely directed (or dictated) from a few urban areas.[1] The United States today is probably as yet the only nation in the world where the ancient gulf between the city dweller and the countryman has been dissolved. Isaiah's complaint no longer makes much sense here, or at least it cannot be understood as a complaint of the country against the city.[2] "Rubes" and "slickers" are no longer differentiated by place of residence. We are an urban people in an urban nation. With the possible exception of people in some of the most remote Appalachian areas and on some Indian reservations, and perhaps with the exception of some of the few remaining black sharecroppers in the South, all of us are to a considerable degree city people in culture, education, and outlook. This development can be understood only

---

[1] One of the interesting and lesser known aspects of mass production is the development of mass taste, brought about by economic concentration and destruction of many independent procedures. When the small manufacturer is no longer able to compete with the giant, due to the latter's greater economy of production volume (and, perhaps, price fixing), the variety of available products declines. This is particularly noticeable in the fashion and clothing industries. It would be interesting to determine the proportion of Americans who are clothed (and have their fashions dictated) by Sears Roebuck and J. C. Penney.

[2] "How is the faithful city become an harlot! it was full of judgment; righteousness lodged in it; but now murderers. Thy silver is become dross, thy wine mixed with water: Thy princes are rebellious and companions of thieves: everyone loveth gifts and followest after rewards: they judge not the fatherless, neither doth the cause of the widow come unto them." [Isa. I : 21-23, AV.]

within the context of the history of the American city and of the three migrations which influenced and directed this history.

The American city of today is essentially a post-Civil War development. The majority of the cities were laid out between 1865 and 1885, following the same architectural patterns (which is why so many of them look alike).[3] Most of them are flat and were built according to a grid pattern of rectangular blocks; their streets were planned to accommodate public transportation consisting of horse-drawn and electric trolleys. Such areas are now the older "inner-city" core of American urban areas. They are surrounded by suburbs of varying ages, as a consequence of post-Second World War expansion (although movement to the suburbs began as early as the mid-nineteenth century with railroad commuting). These older areas of cities are remarkably alike from coast to coast.[4]

The Great Migrations

In addition to their physical similarities American cities are similar in other ways, including their problems, as a result of three great migrations. These population movements, which are among the most significant the nation has known, have determined the present character of the city and the crises which beset it. Only the great move to the West of the last century compares with them in significance. In chronological order, they are (1) the migration from farm to city (which began with the nation's birth and still continues), (2) the black migration out of the South (also still continuing, although there are now

---

[3]   It is not even much of an exaggeration to say that with the exception of our very few planned cities (older Washington, D.C. and New Orleans) and the few where geography has dictated layout (San Francisco and Pittsburgh), all American cities are virtually identical in layout and physical appearance.

[4]   The outskirts of old cities can be located by finding the cemeteries which always surrounded them. These cemeteries were situated at the end of major trolley lines, which, in turn, were on principal arteries.

counter trends to this movement). and (3) the migration from
the cities to the suburbs.

Migration from Farm to City

Cities have been growing for a long while, and much of their
growth has been at the expense of the rural hinterland. After
all, unless urban birth rates are significantly higher than rural
(and they are always lower, as a matter of fact), the population
of the cities must come from somewhere else. Few of us know
the dimensions and the time span of the migration which has
resulted in the urban explosions of the twentieth century. Cities
in the United States have been founded and have grown at the
expense of rural population for at least as long as population
statistics have been kept. A few simple figures tell the story. In
1800 the United States population was 94 percent rural; by
1900 that figure had dropped to 60 percent and by 1966 to 27
percent.[5] Although today approximately one-quarter of the
American people remain "rural" in their residence, less than 7
percent actually live on farms; and not all of those living on
farms are engaged in the occupation of farming. Where have all
the "rural" residents disappeared to? The city, of course. A
similar story is told by another set of figures—the increase in the
number of cities.[6] In the year 1800 there were 33 cities in the
United States; by 1900 that number had increased more than
fiftyfold to 1,737, and by 1960 it stood at 6,841. For the
framers of the Constitution, the typical American may well
have been one of the yeomen who swarmed to Lexington to
confront the British; today the typical American is a city
dweller.

Along with the gross increase in the number and size of cities
there has occurred in this century a change in the kinds

---

[5] According to the U.S. census, *rural* means residing on a farm or in a community
with a population of fewer than 2,500.

[6] Technically, of urban "places." An urban place is simply an incorporated locality
with a population of 2,500 or more.

of cities, perhaps reflecting our increasingly complex technology. A new urban form is emerging. This form has special
problems of its own which are proving difficult to solve for
essentially political reasons. The megalopolis, as this form is
called, is the result of tremendous urban sprawl which has made
"super cities" of our larger metropolitan areas. Thus, the
Greater Los Angeles Metropolitan Area can be said to stretch
from south of San Diego up the coast to, perhaps, Santa Bar-
bara and inland perhaps as far as Riverside or San Bernardino,
while the edges of Chicago's megalopolis range from north of
Milwaukee to almost as far east as the western edge of Cleve-
land. A similar super city will soon exist on the East Coast,
from Virginia to north of Boston and on the Gulf from east of
New Orleans to, perhaps, Corpus Christi, Texas, and inland as
far north as Dallas-Fort Worth. Calling these sprawling urban
areas super cities need not imply that every square mile of land
surface within their limits is built up. It means simply that the
area they encompass is, as a whole, tied to the urban area and
that most of the population engages in urban pursuits. Super
cities pose problems that are different in scale from those of
other urban areas, because they sprawl across several different
kinds of political jurisdiction. No single government controls
their taxation, land use, political activity, and so on; they encompass dozens of police forces and sheriff's departments. If we
count all the water resource districts, fire jurisdictions, and so
forth, many megalopolises include thousands of more or less
overlapping governmental jurisdictions. Thus, although the same
problems may affect the entire area (problems such as organized
crime, fair employment of nonwhites, or pollution), it is extremely difficult to make any kind of concerted attack upon
them, because the tools for doing so are scattered and impossible to coordinate (and, of course, people often have vested
interests in maintaining local control over their affairs).

The significance of this first great migration in shaping the
character of the American city and American life is manifold.
As we have seen, it has increased significantly the number of
cities in the country. It has depopulated large sections of hinterland (there are fewer square miles of land under cultivation

today than there were half a century ago). It has turned the country into a nation of city people and virtually destroyed the small towns throughout the nation which existed as farm service centers. Finally, and perhaps most importantly, it has destroyed the ancient division of the population between farm and city dwellers. Thus, the city in the United States today is in part the product of a great historical (and apparently worldwide) force variously called urbanization, industrialization, or even, on occasion, civilization. Its future is impossible to predict, but it is clear that the city and its future are the products of forces which are not subject to human control to any great degree and which have been centuries in growing. Sociological understanding of these forces will not enable us to influence them very much, but it may enable us to adjust our own behaviors to them.

Black Migration out of the South

As we have said earlier, the black migration from the southern states is the second of the great migrations which has influenced the destiny of the American city and determined the nature of some of its present crises. Throughout the nineteenth century and into the twentieth, the vast majority of black Americans lived in the states of the old Confederacy, as a result of the importation there of Negro slaves. Relatively few black Americans lived in the North or West. But after the Civil War, black people began to move out of the South, presumably to make better lives for themselves elsewhere. In the beginning this migration was largely to the northeastern states. With the industrial expansion during the First World War it shifted to include the Midwest, and with the Second World War the West Coast became another destination. In the 1870s this migration of black people out of the South was a trickle; by 1900 it had become a river and by 1920 a flood. It continues today, although the civil rights and black power activities of the early 1960s have started a small counterflow back to the South. The flood out of the South has dried up in some specific localities for lack of people left to move.

There have been two primary motives for migration—the

hope of escaping oppression and the search for economic better-
ment. The latter has been immensely accelerated in this century
by the mechanization of agriculture, which took away the liveli-
hood for thousands of black farm workers and left them no
alternative but moving to the city in hope of finding employment.

The dimensions of the black migration are best indicated by
census figures. The following table shows the changes in black
population experienced by certain states as a result of migration
in the ten years between censuses. We have included two southern states as examples of out-migration and three northern and
western states as examples of destinations for migrating black
people.

Black Migration (in Thousands)

Source or Target	1890-1900	1920-1930	1940-1950	1950-1960
Kentucky	−12.2	− 16.6	− 22.8	− 15.0
Mississippi	−10.4	− 68.8	−258.2	−323.0
Illinois	+22.7	+119.3	+179.8	+189.0
New York	+33.8	+172.8	+243.6	+282.0
California	+ 9.8	+ 36.4	+258.9	+354.0

Source: U.S. Department of Commerce, Bureau of the Census, *Statistical Abstract of
the United States* (Washington, D.C.: U.S. Government Printing Office, 1970).

An interesting footnote to this table is that as a result of
migration no former Confederate state has ever had an increase
in black population from one census to the next, and no northern or western state has ever experienced a decrease. Although
there is a counterflow of black people back to the South (as
indeed occurs in almost any migration), it remains far smaller
than the mainstream that still runs north and west.

In every case the targets of this great movement of people
have been the major cities of northern, midwestern, and western
states. The reasons for this are economic and technological as
well as purely social. The black communities of the North and

West have always been located in cities; thus, black people leaving southern homes moved to places where other blacks had found jobs and constructed a web of social organization within an otherwise white world. More importantly, however, most of the black migrants from the South were agriculturalists whose skills in southern agriculture had been made obsolete by technology. Furthermore, these skills were inapplicable to northern agriculture (since few northern crops demand the amount of hand labor which rice, cotton, or tobacco do), and in the West and Southwest, native populations of Chicanos and Asians did the necessary hand labor.

Thus, black people migrated to the cities because black communities already existed there and because there was, in fact, no other place for them to go. Only the cities offered an opportunity to earn a living, no matter how poor. The black migrants generally had few of the skills demanded by urban labor markets, so they were forced to become unskilled laborers in an industrial economy that was rapidly rendering such jobs obsolete. This situation contributed far more than its share to the plight of the black population and to contemporary urban problems.

Migration from City to Suburb

The third of the great migrations is the continuing one of middle and upper class people (largely, although not exclusively, white) from the central city to the suburbs.[7] This is not a recent phenomenon, although it has certainly reached flood tide in recent decades. This migration was statistically visible as early as the 1890s, when the invention of the electric trolley car made commuting into the city feasible.[8]

---

[7] Central city refers to the legally incorporated limits of a city, that is, the area within a city's legal limits. An example of a central city is New York City as a political entity; the city and its surrounding area are known as the Greater New York Metropolitan Area.

[8] Contrary to common belief, the contemporary surburban migration is not due solely to the increasing proportions of black people in the cities, although this may

In every decade since 1920 more urban growth has taken place in the suburban fringes around the cities than within the central cities themselves. Since 1960 central cities have experienced an average growth of less than 1 percent per year, while urban areas outside the central cities have averaged about 3 or 4 percent annual growth and sometimes a good deal more. For example, from 1960 to 1965 the Standard Metropolitan Statistical Areas (SMSAs) in the country increased their population by an average of 10.2 percent.[9] But if we divide the SMSAs into central cities and their suburbs, we find that the central cities grew only about 3.2 percent while the suburban fringes grew 17.7 percent. In the same period of time nonmetropolitan areas outside the SMSAs grew only about 3.4 percent, and net urban growth in the central cities from immigration alone was negative. Most of the registered growth of central cities resulted from incorporating surrounding territories. This does not mean that the flight of rural people to the cities had ceased by 1960. The exodus from the hinterland continues, but today it is large-

---

be a major motive. The suburban explosion which began after the First World War and was immensely accelerated by the Second World War is probably rooted in land values. The market price for land is determined by the use to which it can be put. Until very recently the basic formula for urban land prices was simply that the closer one got to the downtown area the more valuable the land was. Businesses requiring large land areas (such as parking lots or used car lots) are rarely found in the central business district, because they do not allow sufficient profit to afford the most expensive urban land. For the same reason, the most expensive plots (those at the principal intersection in the central business district) usually are devoted to financial institutions (banks and exchanges), because they can make greater profit in small space. The high cost of land is probably a major reason for the middle and upper class flight from the city. The cultural values of the "good life" for many members of these classes include owning a home with a yard. Financially, this is a very wasteful use of land, and the land rapidly became exorbitantly expensive as the city's other functions expanded into the old middle and upper class residential districts. Soon the suburbs were the only place where many middle class people could afford to own a home. The current flight from blacks, Chicanos, Appalachian whites, and so on simply overlays and supplants other middle class values and problems.

[9]   We have previously referred to these areas as Greater Metropolitan Areas. However, for statistical purposes the U.S. Bureau of the Census has created SMSAs, which are defined as a county or set of contiguous counties with at least one central city of 50,000 population or more.

ly a lower class and often nonwhite migration. At the same time an even larger percentage of white middle and upper class urban residents are migrating from the central cities into surrounding suburbs. The suburban explosion was accelerated in the sixties by the development of commerce and industry in the suburbs, a result of decentralization and of problems attendant upon urban location of major business enterprises. This has made the suburb a prime target for people migrating from rural areas. That is, people are moving directly from the farm to the suburb instead of from the farm to the city and later to the suburb, as they did in the past.

The Urban Crisis

We have described the three great migrations which shaped the character of the contemporary American city. The social changes caused by these migrations embroiled the city in a series of unresolvable crises which now threaten to destroy it. These changes include rapid growth without necessary planning, as a result of the expansion of industrialization, and greater use of technology in the areas of transportation, communication, and agriculture.

Since the Civil War, and particularly since the First World War, increasing proportions of migrants into the cities have been unskilled members of a rural lower class, often nonwhite. At the same time, major out-migrations from the cities to the suburbs have been made by largely middle and upper class white urban residents. By the 1960s these migrations had produced a serious problem. The central cities had become more or less deserted by skilled workers, whose earnings had been taxed to maintain the essential services and physical plant of the cities. At the same time, the central cities were being filled with a largely unskilled population, whose physical and social needs placed an unprecedented strain on the remaining urban resources. Simultaneously, technological changes were causing an even greater decrease in the industrial demand for unskilled labor, and industry itself, undergoing another industrial revolution, was beginning to move out of the urban areas into the suburbs and rural areas.

More and more, the population of the central cities was being composed of economically marginal workers whose skills were unusable on the only labor market available. The resulting social, economic, and political conditions of these people were made even worse by segregation and discrimination.

The megalopolitan super cities grew rapidly as a consequence of all these factors, and this growth further accelerated the problems of the older central city areas by creating a maze of overlapping political jurisdictions. Even when problems became identifiable, they were often unresolvable; that is, while such problems as unemployment or pollution were universal, the various government units which had to deal with them were all politically limited. This state of affairs has created a national urban crisis of incredible magnitude. A number of analytically distinguishable social problem areas can be identified; but since they are all inextricably interwoven, none can be resolved without the simultaneous solution of the others. To date, this has proved impossible. The principal social problems of the contemporary city are easily delineated.

Finance. The cities are going broke. Most central cities have been running in the red for years, and a few of them are virtually bankrupt. Lenders are declining to offer further aid, and taxes have fallen off because of the flight of the taxable population (both individual and corporate) to suburban areas beyond the city limits. Those living outside the central city commute in to use its resources, and the remaining population is making greater demands on the city's services. Appeals for help to the federal government have been made by organizations such as the Conference of Mayors, but they have thus far largely fallen upon deaf ears.

Education. School systems designed for white middle class children are proving inadequate for the education of poorer and often nonwhite populations. The costs of education have climbed steadily, while the city's tax base has declined. In most central cities the physical plant of the schools is deteriorating (in the older areas many buildings are over a century old). At the same time, the suburbs are using the taxes of the high income urbanites who have migrated there to build sparkling new schools.

Crime.   As the urban population of poor people has increased, the frequency with which certain kinds of crimes occur has risen (without regard to race). As unemployment and under-employment have grown among these urban populations, such crime rates have climbed steadily. The increasing cost of police services and the increasing tensions between police forces (which remain largely white) and the people served by them (who are often nonwhite) have done nothing to alleviate the situation. Neither has help come from the drug plague which has begun to permeate the poorer populations of many eastern cities and which seems to be spreading nationwide, perhaps with the assistance of organized crime.

Housing.   As cities grow older, the original housing deterior-ates. As a consequence both of racial discrimination and of the decreasing average income of typical urban workers, segre-gation, ghettoization, and nonownership of homes have also increased, with yet further consequences for dilapidation of residence units.[10]

Metropolitan services.   With the out-migration of taxable per-sons and businesses, the quality of services offered by the cities begins to decline. The lower quality is found in police and fire protection, health care, education, streets, water, electric

---

[10]   When a population is segregated and economically marginal, it is forced to live in the most dilapidated and least desirable housing areas of the city. At the same time, this housing is very expensive for the individual, since the alternatives available to him are limited by segregation. Furthermore, as a result of the peculiar nature of most American real estate taxation, such housing may be very profitable for the slumlord. He pays little in property taxes, because his buildings are dilapidated; and while he keeps them dilapidated by neglecting all upkeep, he still can charge high rent, because his tenants cannot find other housing due to discrimination. (Such substandard housing often is owned by tax-exempt organizations such as universities and churches.)

power, sewage, and other services. At the same time, the demands for some of these services (such as police and fire protection and health care) actually increase as the city's population becomes more characterized by poverty and unemployment.

We could list many more categories of urban problem areas, but further identification of problems is superfluous to our point. The cities are facing crisis situations of catastrophic proportions; these have been largely unresolvable, mainly because of the interrelationship of all the city's problems. For example, the financial problems of the city cannot be resolved without stopping the exodus of the middle and upper classes and of business as well. But that migration will continue until some solution is found to the problems presented by racial mixture, social disorder, and rising crime rates. These social problems are affected by poverty, unemployment, technological change, racism, segregation, and so on. Some of them might be resolved if the problem of governing the entire urban area could be worked out.

The power of black or other ethnic people to determine more or less what the city does in their neighborhoods will be a hollow victory over the "white power structure" if it becomes only the power to preside over the bankruptcy of the city. Power is politically effective only to the degree that it can affect the basic conditions of life; and the basic conditions which affect life in the central city are those of the megalopolitan area and, as a consequence, of the nation. The problems of racial discrimination and urban disorder are intimately related to the problems of poverty, education, segregation, and housing; these, in turn, are related to politics, economics, history, and psychology. Thus, the crises facing the contemporary American city are interrelated and unresolvable on a piecemeal basis. Since the city is a phenomenon which dominates national domestic life, its problems are national ones and cannot be left to the various cities to resolve for themselves. Indeed, the problems probably are resolvable only at a national level and only when considered as the historical consequence of social change. No resolution of any kind will be possible without recognizing the *social* nature of the interrelationships among the city's problems.

The crisis of the cities is a crisis of caste and class, of social institutions and their responsiveness to great social change, and of changes in the value structure and norms of American society and its subcultures (and the diffusion of these values and norms through socialization). Treating these crises separately or all together but indiscriminately will inevitably result in their remaining unresolved. Only when the problems are understood in terms of the social processes which produce and sustain them, and of the myriad social interrelationships which connect them, can approaches to solutions become possible.

This book has no solutions to offer. But one thing is clear. Without sociological understanding, no solutions are possible. This is the relevance of sociology. There are no easy solutions to social problems; indeed, some may prove to be unresolvable. But no satisfactory solutions at all are possible without acknowledging the social nature of the world within which we live and the kinds of ties that bind us one to another and to the past and future.

Suggested for Further Reading

G. Allport, *The Nature of Prejudice*
James Baldwin, *The Fire Next Time*
Claude Brown, *Manchild in the Promised Land*
Stokeley Carmichael and Charles Hamilton, *Black Power*
Robert Conot, *Rivers of Blood, Years of Darkness*
L. C. Durn and T. H. Dobzhausky, *Heredity, Race and Society*
Martin Luther King, *Why We Can't Wait*
Lewis Mumford, *The City in History*
President's Advisory Commission, *Report of the National Advisory Commission on Civil Disorder*
Arthur Vidich and Joseph Bensman, *Small Town in Mass Society*

Topics and Questions for Discussion

1. Jessie Bernard proposes (*Marriage and Family Among Negroes*) that the social problems of black people cannot and should not be studied as deviations from the white norm. Eldridge Cleaver similarly claims (*Soul on Ice*) that American Blacks have been effectively "colonized" while Martin Luther King maintains (*Where Do We Go From Here: Chaos or Community?*) that Blacks still live under slavery—"spiritual slavery." Using the historical perspective and sociological concepts, explain how it is possible to hold these positions. [Hint: you may wish to consider such matters as cultures and subcultures, deviance, socialization, stratification, urbanization, etc., and consider such things as the fact that whereas whites are usually inculcated in the Protestant Ethic, for Blacks (under slavery, at least, surely), work may have been an evil and was certainly not cherished as a value in itself.]

2. Dateline: April 1, 1971, Chicago *Tribune* . . . "Chicago has until June 15 to come up with a plan to provide 4,300 more low income housing units or it will lose $55 million needed to support the Model Cities and Neighborhood Development Programs.

The plan for the 4,300 units must contain a commitment to build 1,800 new low income units. This can include the 1,500 units now planned for construction by the Chicago Housing Authority at 236 sites throughout the city. The balance of 2,500 units can be supplied either through rehabilitation of existing units or special leasing programs.

The city must submit a program for low income housing that has been approved by the City Council, which means that site locations will have been approved, too."

Assume that one factor complicating Chicago's ability to come up with an acceptable plan by June 15 is that the City Council is divided over the location of the new housing sites. One faction on the Council proposes that the majority of the new housing units be low-rise and be located in neighborhoods that are, at present, predominantly white. The other faction proposes that the majority of the new housing units be high-rise and be built in neighborhoods that are, at present, predominantly black.

Consider and discuss the advantages and disadvantages of both proposals in terms of their viability, implementation, and acceptability to the *groups* involved. *You* have the deciding vote on the City Council: which plan will you choose? (Or would you propose an alternative?)

3. " . . . 'the Negro Problem' is no longer hidden on the plantations of the Mississippi Delta nor in the sleepy towns of the 'Old South' nor even in the bustling cities of the 'New South'. On the contrary, the most serious social problem confronting America today is to be found in the heart of the big cities that are the nation's ornaments. For there is not a city of any importance in the US that does not now have a large and rapidly growing 'Negro Problem.' " (Silberman, *Crisis in Black and White*, p. 7).

Either in aggreement or disagreement with this statement, analyze it from a social perspective.

Bibliography

Nicholas Alex, *Black in Blue*
James Baldwin, *Nobody Knows My Name*
James Baldwin, *Notes of a Native Son*
Milton L. Barrow, *Minorities in a Changing World*
Irving Bieber, et al, *Homosexuality*
Rachel Carson, *Silent Spring*
Kai Erikson, *Wayward Puritans*
Betty Friedan, *The Feminine Mystique*
University of Chicago, *American Judaism*
Oscar Handlin, *The Newcomers*
Calvin Hernton, *Sex and Racism in American Life*
Jesse Jackson (interview) *Playboy*, November, 1969
Robert F. Kennedy, *The Enemy Within*
James Killian, *The Impossible Revolution*
Martin Luther King, *Where Do We Go From Here: Chaos or Community?*
Mirra Komarovsky, *Blue-Collar Marriage*
Mirra Komarovsky, *Women in the Modern World*
J. Kozol, *Death at an Early Age*
C. Wright Mills, *Listen Yankee*
Ashley Montagu, *Race, Science and Humanity*
Lewis Mumford, *The Highway and the City*
Thomas F. O'Dea, *The Mormons*
T. Parsons and K. B. Clark, *The Negro American*
Alphonso Pinckney, *Black Americans*
B. Quarles, *The Negro in the Making of America*
David Riesman, *Constraint and Variety in American Education*
Robert W. Roberts, *The Unwed Mother*
Arnold Rose, *The Negro in America*
Hendrik M. Ruitenbeek, *The Male Myth*
Herbert W. Schneider, *Religion in Twentieth Century America*
Ben Seligman, *Aspects of Poverty*
Edmund Sinnott, *Matter, Mind and Man*
William Stringfellow, *My People is the Enemy*

Piri Thomas, *Down These Mean Streets*
Thorstein Veblen, *The Higher Learning*
Robert C. Weaver, *Dilemmas of Urban America*
Max Weber, *The City*
James West, *Plainville, U.S.A.*
William Foote Whyte, *Street Corner Society*
John Williams, *The Man Who Cried I Am*
C. Vann Woodward, *The Strange Career of Jim Crow*
Malcolm X, *The Autobiography of Malcolm X*
Michael Young and Peter Willinott, *Family and Kinship in East London*

Index of Subjects

Index of Proper Names

Glossary

achieved status

a socially defined role consisting of membership in a social category which may be elected or striven for by an individual. As used in this book, a role which, once achieved, cannot be renounced.

anomie

a condition of normlessness due to lack of understanding, obsolescence or irrelevance of conventional rules resulting in a weakening of social bonds with others.

anthropology

that field of the three general social sciences traditionally concerned with the total study of preliterate societies and of archeology, linguistics, and the physical structure of the human species and its evolution.

artifact

a material culture item; tool, garment, toy, etc. A manufactured or man-produced *thing*.

ascribed status

a membership in a socially defined category which is imposed on the individual by his society and about the acceptance of which he has no choice. Sex and race are examples.

authority

socially legitimized power or ability to influence the behavior of others.

caste

that form of social stratification based on birth in presumed but socially defined categories. Selecting some criterion presumably inherited, such as skin color, a caste system layers all of the members of a society into hierarchial groups (strata) which are then treated as if they were "races" in the conventional American understanding of the latter term. In caste societies most significant social behavior such as marriage and occupation will be ordered by caste rules.

class, social

see social class

consensus

general agreement among members of a group.

constitutive rules

the rules of a game or other system of doing something which define what the game or system *is*. E.g., many games are possible with the small glass spheres called marbles. The particular game to be played in a given instance is defined by (constituted by) the rules.

culture

the designs, patterns, or conventionally accepted definitions of reality and ways of doing things conventionally accepted in a society or social group. Includes the rules for behavior, both those understood as rules and those implicit in "the way things are done," tools and other artifacts, beliefs, etc. Can be used on a variety of levels, e.g., human culture in the neolithic period, Imperial Egyptian culture, Black culture, Southern California beach culture, etc.

cultural persistence

the retention in a culture of ideas and inventions for very long periods of time, as modern American culture still retains the knowledge of how to manufacture neolithic artifacts.

cultural relativism

the belief or proposition that the culture of a people may be understood properly on and in its own terms. For example, the polar eskimo traditionally put their old people on ice floes to die when they became economic liabilities, but this practice cannot be properly understood if it is considered as the equivalent of "murder" in conventional American understandings.

deduction

the logical process of drawing specific conclusions from general propositions or observations.

determinism, social

see social determinism

deviance

variation or departure from a cultural norm. To be understood in two rather different meanings: departure from common practice or departure from behavior in accord with cultural rules or common values. An individual can do either without necessarily being defined as a deviant by others, depending upon the circumstances. For example, to fail to come to an absolute halt at an arterial stop sign is "deviant" in that stopping is what the law demands and one may be arrested for not doing so. To *always* come to an absolute halt, however, is deviant in that most people do not do so in most instances.

dialectic

a concept invented by the German philosopher Hegel describing history as a repeating three-stage developmental process wherein change occurs through the posing and resolution of contradictions or paradoxes.

dysfunction

a negative or unfortunate consequence of what might be in other circumstances a normal or useful practice. For example, the allergic reactions which some relatively few persons have to immunizations.

empiricism

the philosophic-scientific practice or rule of evidence accepting observation of fact as the final authority for the validity of factual propositions; the appeal to the authority of observation or factual evidence as the final determiner of truth.

endogamy

the practice of choosing mates only from within the clan, group, class, caste or society of which the individual is a member.

epistemology

that branch of the discipline of philosophy concerned with knowledge and knowing. The fundamental epistemological questions could be said to be, "How do we know what we know?" and "How do we know that we know what we know?" The concern of this text with sociology as a way of knowing or as a special frame of reference from which to ask questions is an epistemological one.

ethnocentrism

the belief that the ways of doing things peculiar to one's own culture are the only right, proper and moral ways of behaving.

exogamy

the practice of choosing mates only from clans, groups, classes or societies other than the one of which the individual is a member.

folkways

habitual ways of behaving in a society the violation of which
may be noticed by others as ideosyncratic or peculiar but which
will not be punished by them: more simply, customs.

function, latent

see latent function

function, manifest

see manifest function

functionalism

the frame of reference or theory of explanation which
understands or defines a phenomenon in terms of its purpose or
empirical consequences. The view that social or physical
structures are best understood in terms of their behavioral
results. Defining the meaning of a structure in terms of the
behavior it permits, encourages, causes or makes possible. A
functional definition of an auditorium, for example, is that it is
a building which is physically constructed so as to encourage
hearing.

functional imperative

varieties of problems which all societies must solve in order to
persist, for example, food-production and child-rearing.

Generalized Other

a concept invented by George Herbert Mead to refer to one's
internalized perception of general societal expectations for
one's behavior, how "one (anyone) ought to behave."
Analogous to the conscience but not limited to moral matters.

group

three or more people interacting together over time in a regular or orderly way, the basis of which regularity is reciprocated expectations for each other's behavior.

heterogeneity

a condition where members of a given category do not share many characteristics.

homogeneity

a condition where members of a given category share a variety of characteristics.

ideal norm

cultural "oughts"; social rules about what constitutes proper behavior in given circumstances whether or not people actually behave that way.

induction or inference

the logical process of moving to general principles or conclusions from specific observations or propositions.

innovation

sociologically, that form of deviant behavior which finds new and socially unacceptable means to socially specified ends. Crime is the outstanding example in American life.

internalization

the process through which the individual makes cultural norms, definitions and values a part of his own personality structure. The acceptance or adoption of culture. The mechanism through which socialization occurs.

instinct

in strict biological usage, an inherited, invariant pattern of complex behavior followed by a creature without thought as a consequence of his genetic makeup. So far as can be determined, human beings do not possess instincts.

institution, social

see social institution.

latent function

the unintended and/or unknown consequences of a social action or custom. Especially important in understanding the persistence of behavior which appears rationally incapable of performing the purpose for which it is ostensibly undertaken.

law

a special variety of norm found in all societies. Codified in writing or oral tradition, laws are distinguished from other norms by their specific definition of what constitutes an offense, of appropriate punishment for specific offenses, and enforcement by special agencies of the society rather than public opinion or spontaneous collective action.

legitimation

literally, "to make legitimate." The process whereby an idea or act is rationalized as appropriate and proper, i.e., in accord with prevailing norms.

life chances

the probability of given outcomes in life, becoming a physician, marrying a movie star, dying of tuberculosis, etc.

manifest function

the intended consequence of or purpose for which a social act or custom is performed.

model (scientific)

a verbal, mathematical or graphic representation of some aspect of the world as it is or as it might be if stated assumptions were valid. A hypothetical state of affairs describing what is believed to be reality as revealed by specified methods of observation or what would be reality if specified imaginary conditions were true.

mores

customary or habitual rules for behavior which, when violated, are reacted to strongly by observers who respond to a sense of obligation to punish the violater or restore the situation.

neolithic

literally "new stone age"; used in preference to Stone Age or "primitive" as a generic term for preliterate societies. Technically, the latter period of the Stone Age characterized by the discovery of retouching stone edges through pressure-flaking.

neutralization, techniques of

see techniques of neutralization.

norms

cultural rules defining and describing both reality as understood in a given society and proper ways of behaving for most situations. "Rules for the game of life." Includes law, custom, morality, propriety, etiquette, usages, etc.

norm, statistical

see statistical norm

organization, social

see social organization

paradigm

a model or pattern. In sociology a theoretical description of social behavior of some kind consisting of assumptions and deduced propositions.

power

the ability to determine or influence the behavior of others, whether through legitimate or illegitimate means.

preliterate

a society which does not use written symbols, a culture without writing. Conventionally used in social science today in preference to "primitive."

probabalistic thinking

consideration of events in terms of the statistical probability of their likelihood of occurrence or of being associated with specified other events.

proxemics

in anthropology, the study of the ways in which people use and define and react to space or location.

psychology

that one of the three general social sciences which traditionally has concentrated upon the study of the individual and sought individualistic explanations for human behavior, i.e., explanations lodged within the person himself.

rank

a position in a hierarchy of domination and subordination within an organized group. A level of organized hierarchy where the variable structured by the organization is authority.

rebellion

sociologically, that form of deviant behavior in which either or both socially defined means and ends may be subjected to redefinition. Revolution is an example in civil life. The American Revolution, for example, redefined the means to be pursued for the attainment of accepted ends. The Chinese Communist Revolution may be seen as an attempt to redefine acceptable ends through conventional means.

reference group

social groups used by the individual as guides or reference points for his own behavior, groups to the perceived ideals or practices of which he "refers" his own behavior. A reference group may be a social collectivity of which the individual is already a member or merely one with which he identifies psychologically.

retreatism

sociologically, that form of deviant behavior in which the individual withdraws from perceived social demands that he behave in certain ways in order to attain certain goals; a reaction to failure to find socially acceptable means for the pursuit of socially defined goals. Typically, alcoholism, drug addiction, suicide and some forms of mental illness.

ritualism

sociologically, that form of deviant behavior in which the individual, failing to attain the socially-defined goal or reward he perceives as required of him, falls back upon "having played the game fairly," used socially-acceptable means of goal-pursuit, as his defense against recognition of inadequacy. Stereotypically, punctillious bureaucratic demands, following rules for their own sake, etc.

roles

the parts we play in life as actors where the drama engaged in is defined by group memberships. E.g., "father," "teen-ager," "Methodist," etc. Roles are always attached to groups and are reciprocal in that group members have mutually understood expectations for each other's behavior. Many roles are also complimentary, i.e., to be a father, one must have a child, etc.

rules, constitutive

see constitutive rules.

self-consciousness

the awareness of self as an object; the ability to contemplate one's identity or being.

social action

any human behavior which is oriented either directly or indirectly to other persons.

social class

that form of social stratification based on wealth or economic resources (relation to the means of production). Because it is based in an acquired characteristic, a class system typically allows for some vertical mobility—movement up or down in the social structure. In industrialized societies, class is apt to be pervasive and affect almost every area of social behavior.

social control

the means through which a society secures conformity to behavior norms. Probably the most effective of these are the consequence of socialization whereby the individual is taught to want to follow normative codes, but they also include rewards and punishments by external agencies.

social determinism

the belief, view, or philosophical position that human behavior is to some significant degree controlled or caused by social forces, environmental influences, etc., and not subject to the free will of the individual.

social institution

the standard or conventional patterns in which similar groups behave in a given society. The cultural rules which similar groups follow. The commonalities in behavior which one may expect to find among all similar groups. The ways in which groups of a given kind in a society will all be alike.

social organization

the effect of social structure (i.e., the influence of social institutions) in the life pattern of the individual. The ways in which individual behavior "acts out" the social rules which become applicable to the person as a member of a group. For example, "husband as economic support of family" in the United States, an institutional norm, creates a pattern on which individual males organize their lives in order to act as breadwinners.

social stratification

the ways in which given societies rank their members as superior or inferior to one another along some dimension or variable, typically wealth (class), birth (caste), and social value (status).

social structure

the interrelations of social institutions in communal life, e.g., the influence and operation of economic phenomena in religious or educational institutions, and *vice versa*.

socialization

the process through which a person is taught and internalizes (makes a part of himself) a particular culture or sub-culture of which he is or is becoming a member.

sociology

that one of the three general social sciences which traditionally defines its subject matter as consisting of the study of the behavior of social groups and the effects of group membership upon the individual.

Standard Metropolitan Statistical Area

a U.S. Census Bureau term meaning a county or contiguous counties with at least one central city of 50,000 or more in population.

statistical norm

the typical or average or mathematically common behavior in a society, whether or not it is accepted as proper or even acknowledged.

status

a special kind of role imposed on the individual as a consequence of his perceived membership in a socially significant category. The principal statuses are sex, age and race. All members of a society share some aspect of all statuses recognized within it. In the U.S., for example, everyone has a sex status, age status, marital status and race status.

status-achieved

see achieved status.

status-ascribed

see ascribed status.

stratification, social

see social stratification

structure, social

see social structure.

sub-culture

behaviors which specifically characterize identifiable sub-groups within a larger society some of the behaviors of which the smaller group will also share. Within American society, for example, there may be found occupational, racial, ethnic, geographic and other sub-cultures.

system

a pattern of reciprocally interacting structures or agencies which, at least for analytic purposes, may be regarded as closed, i.e., as primarily relating to and interacting only with one another, and which operate to maintain one another. The various organic systems of the body are exemplar: digestive, respiratory, circulatory, etc.

taboo

a special variety of norm distinguished from others by the fact that violation creates feelings of loathing and abhorrence among observers, although not necessarily a sense of obligation to act in order to rectify the situation or punish the violator.

techniques of neutralization

psychological mechanisms used by an individual to convince himself that a deviant act was not truly deviant (wrongful) under the circumstances in which he performed it. A means of psychological self-justification for misbehavior.

values

concepts, goals or activities defined as important in a society—things worth being or doing or having.

virilocalism

the practice in a society of permitting the husband to select the place of residence for the family after marriage. (Not to be confused with patrilocalism in which the newly wedded couple go to live with the groom's family.)